The Robert Tressell Lectures
1981–88

Edited by David Alfred

First published in 1988 by the
Workers' Educational Association
South Eastern District
4 Castle Hill, Rochester, Kent, ME1 1QQ

Photoset in 10/11 Linotron Plantin
by Kench Publishing Services Ltd, Tonbridge, Kent.
Printed in Great Britain by Antony Rowe, Chippenham, Wiltshire
Cover design by Teresa Dearlove

ISBN 0 9508348 1 5

The Robert Tressell Lectures
1981-88

Contents

To the memory of Fred Ball

1905-1988

Written to her mother after visiting Fred Ball in the Chapel of Rest.

No longer warmth excels from that body that I'd kissed goodbye,
Neither shall I see the colour of my father's eye,
Motionless as he lay of innocence and purity.
As dark as night, no longer awaits the dawning of the day.
The parasite of time has crept upon his flesh,
Released his soul and freed his spirit on his day of rest.
The chains of life had captured and tortured his person so,
But in these bleakest hours he's won,
Life had to let him go.

Clare J. Ball

Tribute to Fred Ball

These tributes were given at Bernard Sharratt's lecture on 30 April 1988 at the Falaise Hall, Hastings.

Sadly, this year's lecture is overshadowed by the recent death of three people who, each in their own way, have played an important part in the story of the man whose work we come to celebrate and learn about each year: Raymond Williams was one of the very few – shamefully few – literary critics to have taken Tressell as seriously as he deserves; he was a prolific writer, a famous teacher – he was for a time Resident Tutor for Oxford University's Delegacy for Extra-mural Studies in Sussex, based, I believe, in Hastings – one of the country's foremost intellectuals and probably the leading socialist thinker of recent years: Kathleen Lynn, Robert Noonan's only child, a lovely vivacious woman, whom I had the unforgettable pleasure of meeting on September 18th 1982 – she had celebrated her ninetieth birthday the day before – when Fred unveiled her father's Mural Panel – a very happy occasion: and Fred Ball who, by yet another of those curious twists that mark the whole, long Tressell story, died suddenly on April 14th, just over four weeks after the death of Kathleen, whose obituary in the *Guardian* he wrote.

When I became Tutor-Organiser for the WEA in 1979, I was told that Tressell had had something to do with Hastings (which was in my patch), and a bit later that there was someone called Fred Ball who knew something about Tressell. Although I was already by then a socialist, my knowledge of Tressell's book was virtually nil. That was soon to change when I met Fred, who was then 75. He impressed me straight away with his directness, warmth and wit. I quickly read his *One of the Damned* and was bowled over. Then I read *The Ragged Trousered Philanthropists* and could hardly believe my eyes that such a book could exist: so direct, so humane and so relevant to today.

Fred had, I think, three great roles in life, two of them connected with Tressell. First, his unique achievement, to which we'll always be very indebted, in recovering single-handedly the fascinating story of Robert Tressell's life and manuscript, which began in 1935 when he was thirty and first came across Tressell's book. His record of that story was published first in 1951 in *Tressell of Mugsborough*, now out of print, and then in 1973 in *One of the Damned*, whose 41 chapters include only half of all the information he had so painstakenly collected over a period of nearly forty years.

His second role concerns the manuscript of *The Ragged Trousered*

Philanthropists. By 1946, he had tracked it down – that it should still have existed at all, let alone have remained intact, after all that time was itself a truly amazing thing – and, with six friends, bought the 1,700-page, handwritten manuscript. I'll never forget how he described to me his utter astonishment when he spread the pages on his living-room floor and realised that over a third of the book had been cut from what until then he, like everyone else, had understood was the full, original edition. It then took nine years for Fred to see his aim fulfilled, when Lawrence and Wishart at last brought out the complete, unexpurgated version, the one we know today. In 1977, Fred adapted Tressell's novel for BBC radio's Book at Bedtime.

But Fred had another role that's less well known than the ones I've mentioned. Like Robert Noonan, Fred believed passionately in workers creating their own art and he practised what he preached. Between 1936 and 1950, well over two hundred poems of his were published in the *Adelphi Magazine* (edited by Middleton Murray and Max Plowman), the monthly *Comment, Poetry and the People* and *Seven* (the latter two produced by the Communist Party). Fred also wrote stories which were published in *Seven* and *Breakaway*. 1961 saw the publication of *A Breath of Fresh Air* based on his childhood in Telham. In 1965 it won second place for the Italia Prize (to a book by Robert Graves), and in the same year his novel *A Grotto for Miss Maynier* was published. The BBC also broadcast three plays by Fred and a dramatised documentary based on *One of the Damned*.

I'd like to end by quoting from a review I wrote of *One of the Damned*: 'Fred's style is very individual; crisp, matter-of-fact, witty and often moving. It reflects the man himself; unpretentious, scrupulous and passionate. In his assessment of why Robert Tressell wrote *The Ragged Trousered Philanthropists*, Fred says that, among other motives, Tressell was a writer. So is Fred Ball, and everyone who reads *One of the Damned* will recognise his great achievement'. [pp 12-14, *Our History*, No 7, Winter 1982-3]

Like all of you here and I'm sure many others, I am terribly sad that Fred has died. We'll all miss him very much. It was a great honour to know him. For as long as Tressell lives, so will Fred Ball!

David Alfred

There is a phrase from somewhere in the classics which is often quoted that says, "Let us now praise famous men". We're not here for that today. We are here to praise common men – men who perhaps became famous but whose fame led from their pride in their status as common men. And we remember that 'common' literally means 'belonging to the people'. Two men who belonged heart and soul to the people were Robert Phillipe Noonan, alias Robert Tressell, and his Boswell, Frederick Cyril Ball, alias our late good friend, Fred Ball.

The name of Tressell is old in the history of British socialism, but the name of Ball is even older. I have no idea – and neither did Fred – if Fred was in any way related to Father John Ball, who has some title to be called the first socialist of this island, but it is certain that if the blood and bone of the fourteenth-century priest was not reproduced in Fred then his generous heart and socialist soul most certainly were.

When John Ball stood before the people in those days before the Peasants Revolt of 1381 and said, "My good people, things cannot go well in England, nor ever shall, till everything be made common, and there be neither villeins nor gentlemen, but we shall all be united together, and the lords shall be no greater masters than ourselves", he was echoed by his twentieth-century namesake, Fred Ball.

Robert Tressell and Fred Ball were both dreamers, but neither were controlled by illusions. Their dreams were of things that one day will be, not of things that can never be. Least of all did they have illusions about the working class, which they knew was the only force which could bring their dreams to reality. They knew that workers were sometimes martyrs but seldom saints, only occasionally and reluctantly heroic, but were always a source of hope because of the deep well of untapped creativity which they contained. This creativity, when alienated from them and pressed into the service of the class enemy, becomes a powerful weapon – part of what Big Jim Larkin called the "revolutionary counter-culture of the working class" – a long and almost underground tradition which the Irish poet Tom Kettle called "the secret scriptures of the poor". That tradition, which includes the hedgerow sermons of John Ball, the English Civil War pamphlets of Gerrard Winstanley, the shanties of the seamen, the work-ballads of the farm labourers, mill hands, and miners, and the writings of Tom Paine, was well represented in this century by, among others, Bob Noonan and Fred Ball.

The details of Fred's life are better known to many here than myself. Though we became firm friends over the last twelve years, the name F. C. Ball first became known to me in the '60s when I read *Tressell of Mugsborough*, and later, in 1973, through a Liverpool Trades Council debate on the location of Tressell's grave outlined by the publication of Fred's book, *One of the Damned*.

A few years later I was to become involved in a committee whose aim was to place a stone upon Tressell's unmarked grave. I wrote to Fred calling him 'Mr Ball'. The first line of the first letter I received back from him read, 'Can we dispense with the misters?' It was typical of the man. At that time I knew few writers and thought of them as being elevated and highly self-opinionated characters. Little I've found out since has changed my mind. But Fred was different. He was, I soon found, his own man, with no time for pretensions. When we invited him to Liverpool to speak at the unveiling of the Tressell Memorial Stone, he said, "I don't have to dress up do I? I haven't got a proper suit". I told him that most of the Committee didn't have a proper pair of shoes. Eric Heffer, who represented UCATT on the Committee, insisted that we put him and Jacquie up in a hotel. When he saw his room, he said, "It's very good of you all, but you know, John, I'd have been just as happy kipping on your couch". Neither Fred nor I knew at that time that it would be me kipping on his couch over the following years.

That weekend began one of the most valued friendships of my life, and one of the most instructive. By that time, I'd learned more about Fred by reading his autobiographical novel, *A Breath of Fresh Air*. When you know a writer, it's hard to resist reading his books. This has led me to reading some rubbish in my time, but this time I'd found a gem. It reminded me a bit of *Cider with Rosie* – though Fred's book, while published later, was written earlier than Laurie Lee's. And Fred's writing was less romantically nostalgic. Beautiful though Fred's descriptions of the countryside he grew up in were, he had not forgotten the bone-hard life of the country labourer and wasn't about to let his readers forget either. He makes it clear that the hardness is caused by a class system that cuts off the people of England from the land of England and the things that their labour can make that land produce!

In all he wrote, as in all he did, Fred was a convinced, passionate and lifelong socialist. But I noticed that the 'gentry' in the book were represented, not as one-dimensional bogies, but as real people with their own lives and perhaps their own tragedies. In this Fred perhaps excelled even his inspiration – Tressell – because as a writer as in all else Fred was, as I've said, his own man.

I could talk for longer than the time I have available of my own tales and memories of Fred Ball. Other people have other memories. We have lost Fred Ball, but we'll keep those memories and be better for them. It is right that we remember Fred's years of labour in commemorating Tressell's life and work and in recovering and giving to the world the complete manuscript of *The Ragged Trousered Philanthropists*. It is right that we remember his own writings. It is right that we remember a good friend, and it is right that we should remember him as a comrade. Fred is gone and we all have to come to terms with that loss. I remember some words that Lenin said about the death of a comrade because those words, if true of any man, are true of Fred Ball. He said:

> Man's dearest possession is life and, since it is given to him to live but once, he must so live so as to feel no torturing regret for years without purpose, so live so as to feel no shame at the memory of a cowardly or trivial past, so live that in dying he can say – 'all my strength and all my life I have I have dedicated to the noblest cause in the world, which is the liberation of mankind.'

Finally, I have been asked to convey messages of deepest sympathy and condolences to Jacquie, Fred's widow, without whose help and encouragement none of his achievements would have been possible, and to daughters, Clare, Kay, Jean and Daphne and to all members of his family. The messages are from: Jack Jones (Ex-T G W U), Liverpool Trades Council, Liverpool Labour Party, Ford's Shop Stewards, Liverpool Docks and Waterways and T G W U District and Regional Committee

I am sure I not only echo their sympathy but of everyone gathered here today, and in the time honoured way of the socialist movement I would ask you to rise and observe one minute's silence to the memory of a great man. Thank you.

John Nettleton

Preface

The idea of an annual Robert Tressell Memorial Lecture arose out of the experience of two courses organised in 1980 by the Hastings & St Leonards Branch of the Workers' Educational Association. The first was a day-school on Tressell's life and work given by David Haines. The success of this event helped to pave the way for the setting up of the Robert Tressell Workshop, which went on to write and produce *The Robert Tressell Papers: Exploring 'The Ragged Trousered Philanthropists'*. It soon became apparent that there was a dearth of material on Tressell's book , with the notable exceptions of Fred Ball's *One of the Damned* and Jack Mitchell's *Robert Tressell and The Ragged Trousered Philanthropists* (Lawrence and Wishart, 1969), unfortunately long out of print; there are also a few pages on Tressell in *Socialist Propaganda in the Twentieth-Century British Novel* by David Smith (Macmillan, 1978).

To help rectify the lack of public appreciation of what many people consider to be an important part of our literary and political heritage, and as Tressell was a 'local' writer, I suggested to the Branch the holding of a Tressell memorial lecture in 1981. The proposal was taken up and proved successful. It was agreed to hold another one the following year. And so the tradition was established.

The lectures are published here more or less as they were given. All were taped at the time and transcribed soon after. The transcripts of John Nettleton's and Raymond Williams' lectures were returned to them for completion and minor adjustments, and first published in *History Workshop Journal* (Numbers 12 and 16; Raymond Williams' lecture also appeared in his *Writing in Society*, Verso, 1983). A similar editing process for the other lectures has taken place this year. For this compilation I have made a few, purely technical modifications, naturally leaving untouched the authors' own words and distinctive voices.

For the record, I should add that each lecture was followed by a discussion, sometimes lasting as long as the talk itself. Also, as they progressed, a pattern has developed whereby we try to alternate lectures dealing primarily with either literary, historical or political themes. Obviously these aspects all interrelate and one of the interesting things about the lectures is seeing what connections each author makes. The lectures are presented here in their chronological order. The actual title of the lecture given by Raymond Williams was 'Writing about Working People: the Case of *The Ragged Trousered Philanthropists*'.

1982 was a memorable year for Tressell enthusiasts, as we had the pleasure not only of hearing Raymond Williams in the spring, but also (on September 18th – a lovely, warm, sunny day) of witnessing the unveiling of Bob Noonan's beautifully restored 'Mural Panel' by Fred Ball, in the presence of a large audience, including Kathleen, the daughter of Robert Noonan/Tressell. Very sadly, all three of these leading figures in the Tressell story died earlier this year. I hope they would have liked this collection.

It is with pleasure that I thank all those individuals, groups and organisations without whose participation, encouragement and material and financial support this publication would not have been possible. First, my thanks to all the contributors who have been so friendly and cooperative both at the time of their lectures and during the period leading to their publication.

I would like to express my gratitude to the WEA Hastings and St Leonards Branch committee for all their support and cooperation over the years and for their generous financial backing of this book. I also thank my employers, the South Eastern District, for allowing me the opportunity to produce this book under their auspices.

For their generous financial assistance and encouragement, I am most grateful to South East Arts, to the Southern Regions of the GMB (General, Municipal, Boilermakers and Allied Trades Union) and of UCATT (Union of Construction, Allied Trades and Technicians) and to the committees of the following WEA Branches – Brighton Women's Education, Canterbury, Crowborough, Sevenoaks, Tonbridge and Tunbridge Wells.

The arduous task of transcribing the sometimes not too well recorded, original tapes was most efficiently carried out by Sheila Sexton, Lissette Trembling and Anne Wells. Marion Beeforth patiently word-processed the entire text of the book. I thank all of them for their labours.

I am also very grateful to Jacquie Ball for permission to use a photograph of her late husband, and to their daughter, Clare Ball, for permission to publish her poem.

Readers' Note

Square brackets indicate material added later by the author or editor, including page-references for quotations from *The Ragged Trousered Philanthropists*: in bold type for the Lawrence & Wishart hardcover edition and in roman type for the Grafton Books (formerly Granada: Panther) softcover edition – by kind permission of both publishers.

David Alfred
Brighton
August 1988

Introduction

David Alfred

The lectures collected here take up, often for the first time in print, a wide variety of the many issues arising from Robert Tressell's classic work, *The Ragged Trousered Philanthropists*. The remarkable story of Tressell's life and of the manuscript he left behind is brilliantly recounted by Fred Ball in his *One of the Damned*. In brief, Tressell was the pen-name of Robert Noonan who was probably born in Dublin in 1870. About twenty years later he went to South Africa, where he married and had a daughter Kathleen. In 1901-2 he went to Hastings with Kathleen, having lost his wife. There he worked as a painter-decorator and wrote his book. He died in Liverpool in 1911. *The Philanthropists* – his own abbreviation – was published in April 1914.

An important point needs to be clarified at the outset. The Tressell lectures are not meant to imply in any way that *The Ragged Trousered Philanthropists* is an unflawed literary masterpiece or a sacred socialist text. The claim is only that Tressell's book is, on a number of counts, an important part of the British people's literary and political heritage. Indeed, the lectures may not have been necessary had *The Philanthropists'* long-standing popularity and admiration been matched by its adequate public recognition.

The evidence of the extent of the readership of Tressell's book is remarkable. Based mainly on information from *One of the Damned*, it appears that *The Ragged Trousered Philanthropists* has been more or less continuously in print in Britain since its first publication, through over sixty impressions of three quite distinct editions: the original, 'full' edition, the abridged one and (since 1955) the complete edition. The book has also been published (and translated where relevant) in the United States, Canada, Australia, Germany (pre-war), Japan, the Soviet Union, Czechoslovakia, Bulgaria and East Germany. Conservatively interpreting the phrase, 'scores of thousands' (quoted by Fred Ball) in relation to recollections of the quantities printed of the first abridged edition (1918) and of the Daily Herald Special Edition (also abridged, 1927), and assuming that at least a similar quantity applies to the five Penguin impressions (of the abridged version) from 1940 to 1942, and including information received from the book's two present publishers – I estimate that the cumulative print of Tressell's novel comes to over 500,000: the true figure could well be substantially more.

If one adds to this the many dramatic adaptations of the book from 1927 to the present day and the wealth of anecdotal evidence (such as that recounted in some of the lectures) about its popularity and influence (it is typically a book that is given away or lent and never returned), then it's quite possible that *The Ragged Trousered Philanthropists* has been read by more working-class people in Britain during the last three-quarters of a century than any other book (with the possible exception of the Bible – *The Philanthropists* is, incidentally, known by some as the 'Painters' Bible'). By the same token, it is probably one of the most influential socialists books written in Britain this century.

And yet reference to Tressell's novel-book in literary or political writing is virtually non-existent. Why?

Raymond Williams observed laconically in his forward to Jack Mitchell's illuminating literary study of *The Ragged Trousered Philanthropists* that it 'has been neglected in orthodox literary studies' (p ix). Perhaps Tressell's book is like litmus paper, showing up the ideological orientation of the dominant tendency among the guardians of our literary heritage. Yet, Mitchell, Williams and Bernard Sharratt clearly demonstrate how rich a text Tressell's is and how fruitfully it can be related to the development of English (or British) literature, irrespective of the reader's political views. One is forced to conclude either that the great majority of our literary critics and historians are not doing their job properly or, perhaps unself-consciously, doing their job only too well. It is possible, of course, that *The Philanthropists* is really a very mediocre novel indeed and that is why it has been ignored (with very few exceptions). If a case were made for that, perhaps then an interesting debate would begin.

Given the evidence about its largely 'underground' popularity among workers and socialists, it seems on the face of it rather more difficult to understand why Tressell's book has had such relatively little impact on the intellectual and political development of the labour movement, widely conceived. Perhaps here too the book acts as litmus paper. As Tressell's socialism is based on the unequivocal and wholesale rejection of capitalism, I suppose one may understand why right-wing 'socialist' (or 'social democratic', in the last modern meaning but one, or 'democratic socialist') writers and leaders have kept quiet about Tressell, though it only muddies the political waters that they then insist on thinking of themselves as socialist.

However, it is even odder that the majority of British socialist writers who share Tressell's understanding of socialism have also ignored him. Part of the explanation could be the fact that his book was soon overtaken by the Russian Revolution, since when British socialists have been blinded by it – and by Continental socialist and communist theory generally – to their own native tradition of socialism and radicalism. Another possible reason, applicable also to the Labourist tradition, is that the *The Ragged Trousered Philanthropists* comes in the form of 'literature', which is thought by some to be inferior to 'serious' books or pamphlets or not for 'the likes of us' (as immortalised by Tressell). If only there were more people like Tressell, Fred Ball and Jack Jones who have no truck with workers or socialists who see art – and "all the benefits of civilisation...books, theatres, pictures, music, holidays, travel, good and beautiful homes, good clothes, good and pleasant food", as Owen says (**p 28**, pp 29-30) – as not being for people like 'them'!

Turning to the Tressell lectures, I would like to discuss briefly just a few of the many significant contributions I think they make to our understanding of *The Ragged Trousered Philanthropists.* John Nettleton's lecture, unlike the others, deals with various aspects of Robert Tressell's life (his last days in Liverpool) and a notable chapter of the subsequent Tressell story, in which the author played a major part. This lecture – perhaps one of the finest examples of written Scouse there is – laid a firm foundation for those that followed.

As far as I know, the lectures by Raymond Williams and Bernard Sharratt mark the entry of *The Ragged Trousered Philanthropists* into public literary criticism, apart from the books by Mitchell and Smith mentioned in the Preface, and an essay Mitchell wrote in *The Socialist Novel* in Britain (edited by K. H. Gustav, Harvester, 1982) Between them, they open up many important issues arising from Tressell's book viewed as a literary text. Both authors explain how its title had put them off reading the book, Sharratt going even further, with reservations about its very form as a novel. To some extent, the two lectures show the contrasting preoccupations of different generations of socialist literary critics, as Sharratt explains.

After discussing the various ways in which working-class people have been written about and have written about themselves, Williams focuses on the special features of Tressell's social context which he convincingly argues allowed him to write the kind of book he did. He also talks about Tressell's refusal to accept as given the experience of his fellow workers, but rather seeks, without belittling or denying it – though that does not stop him from lashing them for their ignorance and prejudice – to marry it with an 'understanding of social relations'. Tressell's attitude to the working class is thus far from romantic. Williams combines a stimulating analysis of Tressell's use of language (which Raphael Samuel also touches on, and about which there is surely much more to be said) with what he regards as the lasting quality of Tressell's book, namely its challenge to an ignorance that becomes 'common sense'.

Bernard Sharratt's lecture concentrates on the internal structure of *The Philanthropists* in relation to a crucial question that he believes is linked with a decisive break between the post-1968 generation of socialists and their predecessors who helped to make up the traditional labour movement – Given the development of the novel as a bourgeois literary form, can there be such a thing as a working-class or socialist novel? Arguing that a key aspect of the novel as such is its pretension to truthfulness and not, paradoxically, its fictiveness, Sharratt analyses (as Williams does) Tressell's own Preface and then his opening chapter, 'The Imperial Banquet' (perhaps today it might be entitled 'The Enterprise Culture Banquet'). He shows how Tressell uses a number of literary devices and strategies that novelists have traditionally employed to persuade the reader of the truth of what they were reading. Sharratt then sketches the relationship between truth and 'fiction' in the English novel, from Defoe's *Robinson Crusoe* to Austen's significantly titled *Persuasion*, then in film and now in television. He concludes that, although the novel form contains the inherent dangers of making readers passive and making them accept what they are told – in direct opposition to Tressell's purpose in writing *The Philanthropists* – Tressell avoids them by using two literary techniques that enable readers to judge for themselves the validity of his analysis.

In their lectures, Raphael Samuel and Eileen Yeo discuss two of the most important historical issues inherent in *The Ragged Trousered Philanthropists*, both of which remain central to contemporary socialism: first, the relationship between socialists and the workers whose interests they see themselves as promoting or serving; second, the relation between socialism and feminism (which calls into question the assumption of the first issue).

The heart of Samuel's lecture is an analysis, with a wealth of detail, of the nature and sources of the social and intellectual 'apartness' of socialists such as Tressell and his contemporaries and also those of preceding and succeeding generations. Putting Tressell's socialism into historical context is clearly necessary to help the reader of *The Philanthropists* (particularly if a socialist) to decide how relevant it is to their own time and place. By making the past so vivid, Samuel's lecture implicitly raises not a few hard questions for the present-day socialist. Do socialists think of themselves as an 'elect' or a 'vanguard', or act as if they do? If so, how can they or how should they persuade those whose interests they claim to serve to follow them or their ideas? How far and in what ways are socialists distanced from the working class? Do socialists assume intellectual or moral superiority?

Eileen Yeo also constructively brings the past to the present and, like Samuel, she is sympathetically critical of some of the assumptions of the socialist tradition that Tressell represents. Though he condemned the exploitation of women's labour-power in paid employment, Tressell, as Yeo points out, said nothing about their exploitation in the home. She also observes that the philanthropists' families in the book are much smaller that those typical of such families at the time, which further minimises the reality of women's domestic labour in Tressell's book. In view of his concern to "present ... a faithful picture of working-class life..." (Tressell's Preface), Yeo's point opens up some interesting lines of research. She contrasts Tressell's treatment of women by giving us an account (in her own words) of the life of Hannah Mitchell, a socialist contemporary of Tressell's. This inevitably provokes the question of how much things are different for people like her today. Yeo also places Tressell's views of the relation between socialism and gender relations in a wider historical context, from the early nineteenth century to the present.

Turning to the political dimension of *The Ragged Trousered Philanthropists*, I guess few can read it and not ask themselves whether it is (still) relevant today. There are, I think, two interrelated ways of conceiving its relevance. First, is the structure of British society today basically the same as Tressell described it, that is, is the economy capitalist and is there a corresponding class structure which expresses and supports marked inequalities of power and material condition between people? Second, is Tressell's analysis of the Money System and his belief that its injustice can be remedied only by its socialist transformation valid? Those who believe that Tressell's ideas *used to be* valid but are no longer so have the difficult task – which doesn't prevent them from achieving it – of showing *when* capitalism, social classes and poverty disappeared.

Jack Jones and Tony Benn are in no doubt that Tressell's book is still relevant, in both ways. (It is not a little ironic that the Tressell lectures should have begun soon after Margaret Thatcher became Prime Minister and are being published in the first year of what one might call her government's 'Right New Poor Law'.) They identify many more continuities in British society between Tressell's time and the present than discontinuities, despite all the rapid social and technological changes we keep hearing so much about. Among the most significant are: the continuing role of 'Practical Level-headed, Sensible Business-men', with their continuing congenital inability to prevent social ills, including periodic and long-lasting bouts of mass unemployment, and the continued relegation of this issue in the political agenda; the continuing perpetration of the Great Money Trick; the continuing existence – stubborn and ever-changing in structure, no doubt – of a working class upon which it depends; the continuing ownership and control by capital of most of a greatly extended system of mass communication, one of the main missions of which is to deflect workers from the *real* social 'realities'; and, last but not least, the continuing existence of mass poverty, particularly among the elderly, and such things as still significant class differences in life-expectancy.

As to whether Tressell's belief that socialism provides, at the same time, the theory and the way out of capitalism, Tony Benn poses a fundamental question: Has it been tried? Those who believe socialism equals public ownership, government regulation of the private sector and the welfare state will answer yes. To those who believe these things never jeopardised for one moment the power of capital and its unjust class structure, the answer is no. Willis argues that the existence of nationalised industries offended against the very idea that private ownership and control is intrinsically good. Jones and Benn join him in attacking the attempted return to 'Victorian values', arguing that religio-moral hypocrisy is as susceptible today as it was eighty years ago to Tressell's withering blast. They agree that workers' solidarity is important, but, to Willis and Jones, that Tressell understates it. The lectures by Samuel, Williams and Sharratt provide some clues to the apparent divergence between socialism, seen as an intellectual critique of capitalism, and trade unionism, which has to cope with it. Believing that trade-union and socialist values go together or should, Willis and Jones deplore this discrepancy. Whether the immediate and short-term problems that are the usual concerns of unions can ever be reconciled with the underlying and longer-term problems with which socialists are most concerned is possibly one of the most difficult historic challenges facing the labour movement in any mature capitalist society – from the point of view of those who wish to see its replacement by socialism.

Both Willis and Jones also take up Tressell's claim that workers are sometimes their own worst enemies. Indeed, Jones criticises today's workers – for their ignorance, divisiveness and subservience – in a style reminiscent of Tressell himself, at once honest, angry but in sympathetic identification with those whom he berates. If Jones is right, to what extent should the labour movement be held responsible for not doing enough to educate workers? And how far are deficiences in education (and culture generally), socialism and solidarity related to the divergence between the 'pragmatic' and 'theoretical' elements of the labour movement mentioned above?

Tony Benn praises Tressell for the moral vision of his socialism, pointing out the lack of it among contemporary advocates . This raises issues dealt with in other lectures: for example, the problem of mysticism, which Samuel sees revealed in the last paragraphs of *The Philanthropists*; the problem of communication through a mass media full of 'propaganda and lies', according to Jones; and the problem, as Williams observes, of not falling into the trap of making (or letting people believe that) socialism depend(s) upon people being angels.

One of the aims of this introduction was to show how the Tressell lectures testify to the wealth of *The Ragged Trousered Philanthropists*.

They contain many more points and interrelations than there has been space to discuss. To my mind, the book bristles with a host of interesting issues – many now high-lighted, others waiting to be – that require further discussion. I wonder, for example, what categories of people today's readers of Tressell's novel would nominate to ride in his four 'travelling lunatic asylums' that sped back to Mugsborough after the workers' summer beano? (**pp 494-7**, pp455-8).

Finally, I would like to say something about the present Tressell-WEA connection. By coincidence, while Tressell was working and writing in Hastings, Albert Mansbridge was busily establishing the Workers' Educational Association – to unite Labour and Learning. One of its early mottos was 'Knowledge is Power', very similar to the trade unions' 'Educate, Agitate, Organise'. If knowledge and education have a part to play in the emancipation of workers from what Tressell called 'wage-slavery', is it not imperative that the labour movement rediscovers this truth and aims to realise it, in ways that are appealing to workers? Mansbridge thought that the purpose of knowledge is wisdom and that true education recognises no class barriers. Although his political views were quite different from Tressell's, these beliefs are well-founded, I think, but still wait to be put to the test. Tressell thought that workers cannot achieve self-determination without intellectual independence and self-confidence. It is, therefore, fitting that the WEA should have been a vehicle for helping to bring to a wider audience a better understanding of *The Ragged Trousered Philanthropists* – a book full of humanity – through the Robert Tressell Memorial Lectures.

Robert Tressell and the Liverpool Connection

John Nettleton

28 March 1981, Queens Hotel, Hastings

You just heard it announced that I'm giving a lecture. I'm not a lecturer; I'm a worker. Someone said that I'm a convenor in the Transport and General Workers Union. In three weeks' time I'll be a statistic; I'll be one of the unemployed. I haven't come here today to give you a lecture; I'm not a lecturer. I've come to talk about Robert Tressell.

Why can I stand here today to talk about the Liverpool connection? Because of one reason, a man sitting in the hall today, Fred Ball. He's spent his life researching into Robert Tressell; He found out about the Liverpool connection. So it's with misgiving actually that I'm standing here. I'd rather be sitting down there listening to Fred Ball.

Robert Tressell called his book *The Ragged Trousered Philanthropists*. My talk will be a bit ragged. It will be darting and diving all over the place. But I've never been educated. I'll be introducing Alan O'Toole later on to give a few passages from the book because that's the reason we're here today; to honour Bob Noonan, for Bob Noonan died and was buried in Liverpool. They might have buried him, but they never buried Robert Tressell. He's alive and well, and sitting here today with us.

I'd like to lead into this by talking very briefly about the book. I imagine that everyone in the hall here today has read it – that's why they're here. The book is about a year in the life of a working man, and through that book you can trace the struggle of a worker right the way through from infancy through to old age. The ages in the book range from young Bert to old Jack Linden, and through them Noonan portrays all the stages in the life of the working man from cradle to grave. And through the lunch-time debates conducted by the socialist in the book, Frank Owen, who was actually Noonan himself, he shows the differing political attitudes of the men; of those like Slyme, the paper-hanger, who rejects politics in favour of a religion he does not really believe in, to those like Harlow and Easton who support Liberal and Tory policies which they don't really understand, and whose trust is cynically exploited by people like Councillor Sweater – A-dam(n)Sweater – and his associates who conduct the Council (and it hasn't changed) with almost casual corruption.

By the end of the book, Tressell's characters have suffered every kind of personal and family misfortune at the hands of the System. They support and yet still reject Owen's plea for a more just society. And

Owen, who is dying of consumption, consoles himself with the thought that a similar sickness is eating away at capitalism and there is at least hope for the future. What Noonan did was to portray the entire social system, and the secret of his and the book's success is that he invented nothing. The hell he described was the world he saw and, as Robert Noonan, he was hopelessly trapped.

The secret of *The Ragged Trousered Philanthropists* is its pure simplicity. Karl Marx wrote *Das Kapital*. I've been a shop steward for twenty years. If I were to go on the shop floor and read *Das Kapital*, I wouldn't be a shop steward for long. I'd be out in five minutes. But the chapter on the Great Money Trick is *Das Kapital*, simplified into the working men's understanding. I first heard it when I was on a ship. These few pages are still done at branch meetings and they are still done in what they call the 'hut' at building sites whenever they're rained off, because it is as relevant today as the day he wrote it. I know lads who have got that off by heart. And every new apprentice who ever comes on the building site on the Liverpool Cathedral, that's his first lesson. And he learns that before he learns about the trade; he learns that and that's the way it should be.

I'm not going to say much about Noonan's life because you can read about it in *One of the Damned*. Fred Ball found out that he was born in Ireland in 1870, an illegitimate son of an Irish police inspector. At the age of 16, he left home and he went to Liverpool – and that is the first Liverpool connection. The reason he went to Liverpool was because that was the port where you got the assisted passage to go to America, Canada, Australia and South Africa – all the points of the Empire or associated parts of the Empire. From Liverpool, he set out for South Africa. He showed a very early aptitude for art, so it's quite reasonable to expect that that's why he went into the painting and decorating trade. While he was in South Africa, he was quite successful. In fact, he made enough money to buy himself a piece of land. He even had himself a servant who incidentally was called Sixpence. He might have become a typical colonial, but he started getting interested in politics. In South Africa at that time, as in every other country, there was a lot of other Irish immigrants, and Tressell got interested in the struggle, and during that period he was on the committee of the Irish Transvaal Executive – and don't forget the Irish then as now had no love for the British. Incidentally, one of the committee members at that time was a guy called John MacBride who was later executed by the British by a firing squad.

When he came back to England – we still do not know why – he was in London for a short period. But because of his deteriorating health (he had contracted tuberculosis which in those days was almost always fatal) he decided, for the good of his health, to come down to a place where he thought the climate would be better and that place was Hastings. And it was in Hastings, which he called Mugsborough, that he wrote *The Ragged Trousered Philanthropists*. I don't think that there was any more mugs in Hastings than anywhere else in the country. But the conditions that prevailed in England were different for a working man than they were in South Africa, at least from a white man's point of view. And it was in Hastings that he really got to know them. He got involved with the socialists. [Tressell became an active member of the Social Democratic Federation, the main Marxist grouping of his day.] He started writing pamphlets and at some stage he decided to put them together in a novel – the novel that was discovered after his death and which we know today as *The Ragged Trousered Philanthropists*.

But his health was still deteriorating and he decided that possibly he'd be better off going abroad. So he left Hastings and again went to Liverpool with only one purpose, to make a couple of bob to pay his fare to Canada. But I think Bob knew in his own heart that he was going away to die – and that was the case. Four months after he arrived in Liverpool, he died. All this, plus a lot I've left out, is related in Fred Ball's book, *One of the Damned*.

When Fred's book came out in 1973, it was widely publicised in the socialist movement, possibly more so on Merseyside than anywhere else, perhaps because Tressell was buried in Liverpool. I was a seaman at the time and on the Trades Council and at one of the meetings it was reported that Tressell was in a pauper's grave. Two Councillors, Cllr. Carr and Cllr. Leigh, said they was going to put a monument on the grave. The Trades Council gave them a vote of thanks. But, unfortunately, like a lot of councillors, they didn't know their arse from their elbow. The Councillors couldn't give planning permission because the cemetery belonged to the Church of England.

I came into the picture a little later along with a couple of other lads. I'd left the sea and after a period of unemployment I finally got myself a job. I was elected to the Trades Council again and one of the lads asked me, "Hey, John, check up what's happening on that gravestone". So I checked up and nothing had been done. So the guy I was working with, a guy called Billy Kelly, a great socialist on Merseyside, said to me, "Well, why don't we have a go at putting a stone on the grave?" So I said, "Oh, okay." And he said, "I met a young kid on the dole today who was also interested, who was prepared to give a hand." And that guy was Alan O'Toole. So the three of us met in our house and we formed a committee and decided – finally at last after all those years – to put a stone on the grave.

We thought that it would be an easy and simple job. But like everything connected with Robert Tressell and with his book, there's nothing going to be simple; no-one was going to do no favours. We wrote to the Church of England. At first we contacted the local parish church, St. Nicks, and we went down and we saw the guy there and we told him we wanted to put a stone on Robert Tressell's grave. So he asked who was Robert Tressell. So we told him and he nearly collapsed. He said, "Oh, you can't do that; you need permission from the Church of England, St Martin's-in-the-Fields." So we wrote to them and they said, "No, it's impossible."

There's a saying in Liverpool, 'everything's possible'. So we asked the fella from the Church of England what law there was that said it was impossible. There's no such law. So then he tried to give us what we call in Liverpool the 'bum's rush'. He said, "We'll give you permission if you get the permission of all the living relatives of all the other paupers in the grave." And some of the names of the people in the grave is called Davis and Davies. Now, Liverpool is known as the capital of Ireland. It's also the capital of Wales. There's about thirty pages of Davises, and they're only the ones on the telephone. So we sat back for six months and we sat in our house and wrote all these letters giving permission and we sent them back to the Church of England. We said we'd done all this research, we checked it all out, we'd got an army of researchers all over Merseyside. It took us six months. They couldn't prove it was untrue because they'd have to do all the research what they asked us to do. So then they said, "It's not up to us; it's up to the fella in Liverpool." We'd been to him years before. So we were back to square one.

The next thing, it was in the the *Liverpool Echo* (it's worse than the *Obscurer*) that there was a new rector taking over at St Nick's, or St Nicholas's as it's really called, in a fortnight's time. So when he arrived, this rector, we were sitting on the step waiting for him. But we wasn't falling for the three-card trick no more. We wasn't going to tell him that Tressell was a socialist. We said, "Look, there's a guy buried there: he's a poet and he's in the same mould as Edgar Allan Poe and Shakespeare and we want to put a stone on his grave. And not only that, we want to clean the mess in the cemetery that the vandals have made. And we've got a job creation scheme and we want to do this up, rosebuds and bushes round the cemetery, clean the graffiti up and everything." He welcomed us in. He thought we was mad doing it for nothing. "Come in lads, have a cup of tea and biscuits", he said. "Well, let me check up,"he said. "You'll have to pay the entrance fee for the Church – £36". Luckily the lads had been paid that day (I was only on about £48). So I said, "There you are, there's the money. Sign that." So he signed. So we had the permission, didn't we? That was it. That's all we needed. So we said, "Before anyone finds out what's going on, let's get the stone on that grave."

So we sat in our house and we decided to form a committee. We put on the likes of Jack Jones, the head of the Transport and General, a personal friend of mine, and Eric Heffer and a lot of other people who we knew would support us. Then we called a press conference announcing our intentions.

Well then we sat down and thought, "What kind of stone are we going to put on?" and we got in touch with the guy who we thought should be consulted first. And he's here today, Fred Ball, and Fred said, "If there's a stone going on there, it should include the names of all the other paupers." So that was done.

We decided the stone should be vandal-proof – we knew the National Front would have a go at it anyway. So we ordered the stone – we never had a penny, never had a light – from Sweden. And we contacted the trade union movement in Sweden. It had to be only trade unionists working on that stone. Then we brought the stone from Sweden through the National Union of Seamen over to Hull; and the Hull lorrymen took the stone with trade union drivers to Aberdeen; and the lads in Aberdeen who polished the stone were trade unionists; and the Liverpool drivers who brought it down were all trade unionists; and the guy who worked on the stone was a trade unionist – we wasn't having no scab working on that stone.

And we still never had a penny. So then we launched the appeal. We got an immediate response from UCATT, the building workers' union. The stone cost over £1,000 – "We'll pay for it." Then Jack Jones wrote back saying, "I haven't had the chance of seeing the Executive, but you will get a donation" – that was the Transport and General Workers. And the National Union of Seamen sent £100 and someone else £100, pensioners and people from Australia, and Japanese yens and Yugoslavian dollars. We had more money than we wanted. We decided that the rest should be used in carrying on the fight to get Tressell recognised, and we've done quite a few things since then.

That wasn't the end of the story. Although we had permission to build a stone, we didn't know the exact place in the cemetery. In Fred Ball's book there was photo of a jam jar took by the BBC. Mrs Marsden, who was superintendent when the TV cameras came down, she said, "He's over here somewhere," and they just put a jam jar down, focused on that and said, "That's his grave." But we found out from an old grave-digger that the way they marked out the paupers' section was that they had an architect's mark and they run out a plumbline. And he also told us that paupers were buried different from anyone else; where an ordinary grave had four foot between, a pauper's grave was six foot by four foot and only two foot between. And you know what they done? They used to bury them in the opposite direction. They worked them to death, and then they used them as a drainage system after they died.

So we finally found the general direction. But it was overgrown wasteland with grass about three foot high. And we'd been searching for quite a few months up and down looking for a small sandstone marker, and we couldn't find it. And we were up the wall. It was the summer a few years ago, 1976, and we had a heatwave up in Liverpool; and I was with Billy Kelly, and we were going along the railway embankment and a spark had set fire to the grass. And Billy said, "Wouldn't it be lovely if we was looking there?" So I said to Billy, "Hey Billy, you'd better go to the library and change your books." And when he came back, there were three fire engines – and I had no matches. Well, we said we'd tidy the cemetery up. We found the marker three weeks later.

Another thing that happened during that period – and there's a lot of stories that I could tell you about it – but one that's always stuck in my mind is that whilst we were looking through this long grass, there was IRA prisoners in Walton jail which is right opposite the cemetery, and they found some explosive outside the jail. So there was top security on, and they had cameras, the lot, and, as I say, where he's buried is right close to the jail. And Billy Kelly was looking through the grass, and as he was coming out of the cemetery, two cars came up on the pavement, pinned him against the wall. And these six fellas jump out the car – you know the style; broken noses and bent ears – "Stand over against the wall" and hands were across his throat. "What's your name?", he says. "Kelly." He said, "What are you doing in the cemetery?" He said, "I'm looking for Noonan," and before he could explain he said, "Your name's Kelly and you're looking for Noonan? Now come on, who else is with you?" He says, "We've got a committee." "On the committee", he said, "there's myself and there's O'Toole." They had heard enough; they took him in. We had to do some explaining to get him out.

Finally, we did put that stone on his grave.

But the work that we said at the time we'd carry on, we did, and took up from where Fred Ball left off. We decided to research Noonan's last few months in Liverpool. When you've read *One of the Damned*, you'll know that he took lodgings at the house of Mr James Johnson and his wife, Mary Anne. The house was 35 Erskine Street. It was a modest enough building, but even so the rent must have been difficult to raise for a labourer. And Johnson must have supplemented his income by using it as a lodging house, as did many others around the same area. The area was well known as a dwelling place for building workers in those days when the so-called 'tramping system', whereby workers would be assisted by the union to travel the country in search of work, was still in force in the building industry. And it seems fair to assume that the local branch of the Painters' Society recommended that address to Bob Noonan as a place where good and economical lodging could be found, though whether he would have received financial assistance from the Society remains uncertain.

It's interesting to note that Bob's sister Ellie lived in Liverpool, but it's not been possible, although we tried, to trace her descendants; and it's not possible to say whether, at any time during those last few months, he had actually got in touch with her. That he didn't stay with her is suggested since it's well known that there's never any love lost between Bob and certain members of the family who were rather conscious of their status as the children of a baronet and felt that he had rather let the side down by becoming a working man.

So, what can we say about Noonan's stay in Liverpool? The answer is, very little. The four months of the stay, prior to his admission to the infirmary, are a mixture of mystery, rumour, legend and a few established facts.

In 1910 Liverpool was in a state of depression which, in the space of a year, was to lead the city into a massive strike movement. Being a rich city, nonetheless, Liverpool could afford to run no less than five workhouses, all of which were filled to peak capacity. And I presume the building industry felt the effects of the recession, and Bob may have had difficulty in finding work. There are several stories of his working. One is that he worked for Joseph Faircloughs, a builders in Juvenal Street, quite close to Erskine Street. Faircloughs seem to have done a big trade in engraving copperplates – which were a speciality of Noonan's – which was practised in a lot of builders during that period, including Adams and Jarrett for whom he worked in Hastings. So the story seems likely enough. Unfortunately, Faircloughs haven't preserved their records from that period, so the story can't be confirmed.

Another story has him working at repainting the emblems of the Liverpool Tramway Company, and the reason why that story has been in circulation for a long time is that, at that period, they was changing over from the old private tramways into the municipal, local corporation trams. They was changing all the emblems, and signwriters and people who could do that artistic work, which was all hand-painted in those days, there weren't many around on Merseyside, so it's quite likely that he could have been employed because of his skill. Again, whilst this is a popular story among Liverpool painters and could be possibly true, the appropriate records are unobtainable. One avenue of research would be the records of the Painters' Society, now incorporated into UCATT, but, sad to say, these records have not so far been traced. Nor is it certain that Noonan was a member of the Society in any case.

And what of Robert's other movements during this period? Here again we are almost entirely in the realms of rumour and speculation. At the bottom of Erskine Street is a long street called Islington which leads into the city centre. The road junction which begins at the top of

Islington is called Islington Square and it eventually became known as Red Square. There's a cafe there that is most frequented by the local building workers, and, since he only lived round the corner in Erskine Street, we can well imagine Bob walking down to the cafe for his evening meal and then listening to the speakers. One small piece of confirmation lies in a family tradition passed on to Billy Kelly (who was a member of the Liverpool Memorial Committee). Billy Kelly tells us about his uncle, who was a pavement artist and used to do a lot of pavement work on Islington Square, who met a man who talked to him about his paintings. Years later, on seeing a picture of Robert Tressell, he came to believe, and remained fixed in his belief throughout his life, that his conversation partner was Robert Noonan.

If Noonan had walked along the length of Islington into the city centre, he would have come to the 'Clarion' cafe in Lord Street. The Clarion named after Robert Blatchford's pioneering socialist newspaper, ran a tea room; and we can well imagine Bob visiting this spot and conversing with the local socialists. One famous spot for the local socialist orators in Liverpool in that period was the so-called 'Edge Hill Lamp' where a meeting would be held every night at a street corner of that name. Again, this was only a short distance from Erskine Street. But what we do know is that Bob attended. Fred Bower, who wrote *Rolling Stonemason*, one of the most well known Liverpool socialists at time and himself a worker-writer, recalls being approached after giving a talk at the Edge Hill Lamp by a short, dapper man in a grey suit who congratulated him on his speech and said, "They'll come round to our way of thinking, eventually," and then left. A friend of Bower's told him that the man in grey had written a book called *The Ragged Trousered Philanthropists*. The only man in Liverpool who could have known of the authorship of Tressell's unpublished manuscript was S.H. Musten, a Sussex syndicalist, recently arrived in Liverpool from Hastings, who Tressell would almost certainly have known. And, since Musten was a close associate of Bower's, it seems reasonable to assume that he was Bower's informant.

By far the most interesting story of Noonan in Liverpool is that he himself conducted an open-air meeting at the Pier Head. The claim is made by Robert Quigley, later a personal envoy of the IRA leader, Michael Collins, who visited Liverpool in 1910, apparently to confer with the Liverpool Irish Nationalist Party. Quigley recounts that, while he never spoke to Tressell, he could clearly remember hearing him speak at the Pier Head, but he found out who Tressell was a couple of years later.

After that, the next we hear of Noonan is being taken to the Royal Infirmary, which was the workhouse in those days and that was in Pembroke Place. The day was November 26th 1910 and the significance of that date is that, on that day, Tom Mann, Fred Bower and others founded the Industrial Syndicalist Educational League to spread the gospel of the doctrine of direct action for socialism throughout the lecture halls of the country, a project, as Fred Ball says, which must have been dear to Noonan's heart. After this, we hear of him being well enough at Christmas to help to repaint the wards (recounted in *One of the Damned*). On the morning of February 3rd, 1911, he died, the cause being cardiac arrest due to phthisis or pulmonary tuberculosis.

Some of the stories which have been told of Tressell today in Liverpool can't be verified. All that can be guaranteed is that they tend to be told whenever Tressell's name comes up in socialist discussion, as it so often does on Merseyside. And in one sense, it doesn't matter if they are true or not, because legends are really stories which people tell themselves because they may be more true than the truth itself. It may be that these stories are an attempt to flesh out the bare bones of the Tressell-Liverpool connection and to make him seem more a citizen of Liverpool, the recognition of the great role he and his book have had in developing and shaping the political consciousness of the Liverpool labour movement.

The book has had of course, as I've said, a great effect on the trade unionists in the Liverpool building industry. Among the painters of Merseyside, as everywhere else, it is universally read, but also by other sections of the working class; and it's used extensively on on-site meetings and in study groups. Possibly the most well-known trade unionist to come from the ranks of Liverpool, or to come from the ranks of the Liverpool building workers, was a guy called Leo McGree, a joiner and official of the Amalgamated Society of Woodworkers. Leo McGree became one of the most famous, well-liked and hardest fighting trade unionists in Liverpool during the 'twenties and 'thirties and, despite frequent clashes with his union leadership and with the Trades Council, virtually dominated the Liverpool labour movement until his death in 1966. Jim Arnisson, in his recent biography of Leo, acknowledges Leo's debt to *The Ragged Trousered Philanthropists*, his bible, and would often quote it in his speeches.

Outside of the building trades, we might think of Jack Jones, who started his career in Liverpool as a docker and who said of his experience of reading *The Philanthropists* as a young lad: 'I couldn't lift my eyes from its pages. It was so real in its exposure of much of the life around me which I was beginning to experience in my first job. But the great significance of the book for me was the simple, clear explanation of the nature of socialism. The inspiration to become involved in the great cause of Labour was overwhelming.' This list could be multiplied many times, not only with the famous but with the thousands of rank and file militants who make up the backbone of the movement. It's a common saying in Liverpool socialist circles that for every person brought into the movement by Marx, there's ten brought into the movement by Robert Tressell.

A few weeks ago, I got asked to go to Rochdale to speak to some textile workers in a factory that was getting closed down. And after it, I went back for a cup of tea with this fairly old lady who'd been a shop steward for thirty-five years. And in a typical Lancashire house they had what we call the front parlour where they had the old china and all their worldly possessions. And they had the old china case there with the best tea cups in. And in this cabinet there was a record, the first record of Gracie Fields – our Gracie in Rochdale, as you know, a living legend – and there was this record of Gracie Fields and there was this well-thumbed book, *The Ragged Trousered Philanthropists*, and we were talking and her husband says, "If the house went on fire and you could save one thing in the house, what would you save?" And this old woman, she looked at the Gracie Fields record and she looked at *The Ragged Trousered Philanthropists*. She said, "'Fraid our Gracie will have to be cremated."

In 1977, a Liverpool trade unionist named Tony Bradburn visited the still unmarked grave lying between the derelict cemetery chapel or church (whatever you call it) and the overhanging towers of Walton jail and, while he was standing there, he wrote a poem and he called it 'Upon a Visit to the Unmarked Grave of Robert Noonan' and it goes like this:

Wintry roots comfort the workhouse waste
Forgotten men and women bone to bone
Briars, weeds, bare shooting canes and dank earth
Entomb the source of Noonan's self-erected stone.
A desolate church, a man-made shell, turns
Aside from the prison towers.
And each in turn think they've claimed his soul
That escaped in the darkest hours.

I think, to wind up, I'd like to give a little piece that I wrote; it's satirical, it's typical Scouse, but it sums up to me what Tressell was writing about. It goes like this:

It was crisis day in the Council
And the chamber was hushed and still,
When Grinder rose with a question:
Are we doomed to go downhill?
The chamber was hushed and silent
When Adam Sweater made reply:
If workers keep their pay at bay,
We'll all be home and dry.
How true, how true, cried Misery,
Let's end this wicked strife.
Here, here; here, here, cried Easton,
They can stick it where they like.
Thank God, thank God, cried Didlum,
There's faith on the factory floor,
And now we got this extra lot,
We'll give it to the poor.
They ran amongst the workers
And the paupers without a fuss,
Handing out the money, saying,
Take it; you need it more than us.
And Mugsborough was filled with singing
And old Joe Philpot's laughter spread,
As hand joined hand in the golden land
And pigs flew overhead.

The Ragged-Arsed Philanthropists

Raymond Williams

23 May 1982, Queens Hotel, Hastings

We are meeting today to celebrate the writing of the *The Ragged-Arsed Philanthropists* for three reasons. First, because the composition of that quarter of a million words by a signwriter and decorator, often working up to a 56½ hour week, remains extraordinarily impressive. Second, because after its all too probable initial rejection, it made its way, first to what is often called the 'abridged' but is more properly the 'reduced' edition, and then, largely through the sustained and devoted work of Fred Ball, who I am pleased to see here today, came through very much in its original terms. And third, because we can now see it in the context of a growing body of working-class and socialist writing, which at once is a body of achievement and sets quite new problems of analysis and context.

But first, the celebration, and you will notice that I took the title which, it's a fair guess, would have been preferred if there hadn't been the restrictions which Tressell mentioned in his short preface on what he dared to write within the conventions of the time while still giving a faithful representation of the language of working people. I have a sore point about the title because I was prevented, for many years, from reading this extraordinary book in its then reduced edition because I took it, from knowledge of its title alone, to be one of those maudlin Victorian tracts which showed that it didn't matter how poor you were, you could always help others, and I'd assumed – I suppose I shouldn't have – that it would be a sentimental tale of people down on their luck who were helping others, which was one of the forms of evasion of social and moral questions which were standard in Victorian writing addressed to working people.

The savage irony of the title could never have been missed if the true sense of what was being talked about – 'The Ragged-*Arsed*' – was there and explicit. We shouldn't, of course, now, change what Tressell had to call it, but it is useful for a moment to think of the difference because it raises the first of the problems. One of the problems all through has been whether working people are a proper subject for fiction. You have to get some historical perspective on this, and it's comforting in one way to realise that, as late as the 1830s, middle-class people were still wondering whether they were interesting enough to have novels written about them. Still in the 1830s, the preferred material of the novel was either something wholly exotic, in the literal sense of being about adventures in other parts of the world, or about the aristocracy – the loves and romances of the aristocracy. And this, oddly, though it is the way a culture often works, was still dominant at least a century after important middle-class fiction had begun to be written. How to believe, at that time, that there was important material in the lives of people who spent much of their time in work, which was as true of that new small bourgeoisie as it was later true of the wage-earning class who were the next fictional stage – that was the question. Would *work* be interesting enough, would *shops* (as, a century later, Virginia Woolf was still wondering) be part of significant life? Eventually, of course, some of the major classics of the Victorian novel were made out of the daily substance of that kind of middle-class life, though still with older and residual preoccupations about the inheritance of property, about advantageous marriage and so on. That new life broke through and if we look back at what we are increasingly discovering, the number of articulate, literate, energetic, highly intelligent working men and women – all through, but we know most about them from the mid-eighteenth century – the astonishing thing is that this different area of society didn't get written about earlier and particularly in the novel which was then the most widely distributed popular form. In general it didn't, although we are still discovering a few isolated and largely forgotten working-class novels from the nineteenth century, just as there has been a steady discovery of what preceeded them, a large body of working-class verse from the mid-eighteenth century and again (and these may be, in the end, almost innumerable) working-class autobiographies, direct stories of their own lives by working men and women.

We can now see that autobiography was the more accessible form because there was a basic lack of fit between the shape of working-class lives and the inherited forms of the novel. This was true even of middle-class lives because even there, and to a much greater extent in the working class, the inheritance plot and the marital property-settlement, which between them furnished eighty to ninety per cent of the basic plot structures of the nineteenth-century novel, were largely irrelevant. So there was a certain nervousness about the novel. If the novel had to be about things like that, then any other kind of material had, so to say, to be inserted, apologised for, transmuted in some way. The autobiography was a more directly accessible form, but itself with problems. On the one hand, there was a tradition, very available to the organised working class of the nineteenth century, of religious witness, especially in the Nonconformist churches, in which somebody described his experience to justify his beliefs. This passed directly into certain kinds of political writing, the tract and the pamphlet, but also stayed at the level of autobiography as in Samuel Bamford. This is writing which depends on the tradition of witness – 'I am like this because I have lived like this' – and then in the description of 'living like this' comes a condition which is not only personal but that of a whole class, a whole people.

But there is another less favourable precedent for autobiography, evident in all too many nineteenth and, of course, twentieth-century examples of the story of the man who has risen out of, or through, his class, who could use the autobiography precisely to show that he was an *exceptional* person. This produced that structure which persists in a lot of working-class writing of every kind, in which working-class conditions are the early chapters – 'My Life and *Early* Hard Times' – as a preparation for the climb-out to the Peerage, the Membership of Parliament, the leadership of one of the great Unions, Chairman of one of the great Companies. And these things happened.

The tone of some of the worst examples is extraordinarily odious but, on the other hand, even given what we now know about how many working people were writing, they were all likely to be – in the human sense, not in the false sense of social privilege or honour – exceptional people. They would be exceptionally stubborn and persistent. They would have exceptional energy and often exceptional gifts. And for these different reasons, the form of the autobiography, for a very long time, absorbed the translation into writing of working-class experience instead of the novel. Moreover, there might be a further reason, in the hardest times, in the simple conviction that the truth had to be told and truth, within a positivist culture, seemed to belong to documents rather than to what was called 'fiction', although both really are matters of writing, and truth is only rarely determined by those generic choices.

So the importance of Tressell's work lies not only in the fact that he broke through to the novel but that he broke through to it in spite of these real difficulties. In his striking, original way he broke with precisely the inherited assumptions of what it was to write a novel, and to write a good, competent novel: assumptions which were very strong at those key points where he was engaging in his own real material.

There are three ways, when you come to think of it, of writing about working-class lives. The dominant one throughout has been the novel centred on the working-class *family*, for which there is much formal precedent. For it is only a step, usually a conscious step, from the kind of family novel through generations of middle-class life, which was written over and over again in the nineteenth century, to the novel of working-class life in which the family is presented, lived with, lived through, with more general conditions arising naturally as the circumstances of that family, or with some of the great crises of working-class experience happening to that family, often disrupting it. There are some major examples in Welsh working-class writing including those in Welsh like that remarkable novel by T Rowland

Hughes, *Chwalfa*, about the North Wales quarrymen, or the novel about mining life like Gwyn Jones's *Time like These* where the writing is composed around the very close family whom you get to know close up as people. Thus a familiar fictional transition happens at once, and yet this is a family living under pressure and usually hitting crises. Again and again the crisis of this kind of novel is the major strike, typically those of the appropriate period, the strike of 1926.

Then there is the attempt to move beyond the controlling fictional form of the family in that difficult transition, even at times ambiguity, between working people and working class. For the class is a matter of consciousness, the class is a matter of organisation, the class is a social reality and yet at the same time it is not necessarily a social reality which exists in anything like the way in which a family does. To speak of a working-class family can be simply descriptive. To speak of the working *class*, that is different; although there is some overlap. Because what is then being looked at is the life of people defined not only by the kinds of work they do or by the fact that they have families and the ordinary crises of life, but by the fact that they have come to see something common in their situation which they call class, which is either their explicit organisation – and it's usually easier to do at those very articulate and organised moments, hence the popularity of the strike, the dispute, as ways of showing them as a class operating collectively – but which is there in another sense, yet often ambiguously or with great difficulty, often being the very question which people are asking or which some inside the class are asking other members of the class who may refuse the description which is being offered to them. No such condition is as physically available as a family. So, if we're talking about working-class crises in the strictest sense, there's this new problem in fiction which didn't touch middle-class writers in the same way, since their dominant consciousness was from the beginning posited on the notion of individuals and their immediate primary relationships. What the most engaged working-class writers had to face was the new problem of showing whole, determining social relationships.

It is at this point that a lot of recent argument has gone round and round and at times got stuck. To show whole, determining social relationships requires a new perspective and this perspective is best known in its more generalised and abstract forms. Moreover, the best known of these forms is socialism and once you arrive at that, quite apart from the familiar difficulties, you soon get told that if it is a novel about socialism it is about something which is not manageable in fiction at all. This is the familiar doctrine of orthodox criticism, which attempts an *a priori* rejection of ideas and movements as the materials of imaginative writing (even after *War and Peace* and *The Devils*). But then the interesting thing about Tressell is that he did write about a wage-earning family; he did write about its relation to a class and to the consciousness of the class; and he did this not only positively, but also in terms of its absence, yet the absence defining it in another way, the absence of that conciousness in a sense defining the question.

The three kinds I've described – the family novel, the family novel partly extended to a class and the novel written from a conscious class perspective – do not easily overlap or integrate because the work is set on different bearings from the beginning according to which of those emphases the writer is most interested in. Yet if you look in Tressell's preface you see, first, '...my intention was to present, in the form of an interesting story, a faithful picture of working-class life'. This indicates a realist version of extending the family novel, its extension to many working people. Then you get: 'I designed to show the conditions resulting from poverty and unemployment: to expose the futility of the measures taken to deal with them...' He is moving rapidly now to the sense of a new perspective, and he adds: 'and to indicate what I believe to be the only real remedy, namely – Socialism'. He was then worried because, in received terms, he was writing not a treatise or essay, but a novel. So he went on: 'My main object was to write a readable story full of human interest and based on the happenings of everyday life, the subject of Socialism being treated incidentally'. This is pulling back from what he had earlier said, but of course it is just where the problem is, and not only for him but for many others. It is a problem of writing, but as such, in its fullest sense, it is also a problem of social and historical consciousness. This requires some more general consideration.

If you look at the history of working-class writing, you find, as indeed you find in more directly political manifestations, that there does seem to be a problem of correlation (which some of us for theoretical reasons used to be rather unwilling to acknowledge) between working-class life in its simplest descriptive sense, that of wage-earning, primarily manual workers, and the degree of combination or concentration which is usually a factor of the nature of their labour process. And if this is so, it follows that you cannot begin to discuss the problems of working-class writers without defining – here or there – what kind of working class.

If you go back to the nineteenth-century middle-class novelists who wrote about industrial life and who included often sympathetic,sometimes distorted but very responsive material from their observation of working-class life, you will find them looking first at the textile mills, where a new form of social organisation was visibly and dramatically present, so that instead of the old conditions of scattered hand-work where the workers might never be more than twos or threes, or a dozen or twenty at most, or would even still be working in homes inside the family, suddenly there was this new, vast social innovation of hundreds of workers under the same roof. This life in and around the textile mills accounts for more than three-quarters, I would say, of that early writing which acknowledged the existence of working people. They were the visible minority in what was of course in general the great majority of wage-earning people in the culture and society that was producing this writing.

And then if you go on you find that there are kinds of labour processes which need a certain significant kind of close, even closed, community. And you find also that it is these communities which have been most prolific over a run of time, to our own day, in producing working-class novels – the mining areas, whether the coal-mining areas or the quarries; or the tailoring sweatshops; or the shipyards or the docks – places where you are simultaneously a working man or woman, a member of a working-class family in the simple, descriptive sense, but also a member of a working-class community, often almost wholly a working-class community like a mining village or a dockside urban district or a shipbuilding area or a textile town. Moreover, these communities exist in a particular part of the country, Welsh or Geordie or Cockney or Clydeside, and because of this the whole spectrum of social relations comes at once in an integrated form. You only have to step outside in the street to be in a working-class community and then within that very intense, often one-track community, the problem of class, which would in more mixed communities be subject to much more complex interpretation, arrives enmeshed with what is also your identity as the people of that place and the people of that region, for you belong simultaneously, over the whole range.

There is then a positive correlation, of which can there be no doubt whatever, between places of that kind and the development of working-class political ideas. Still any political map of the country will show you that it is in the places where such labour processes created working-class communities of that kind that the great institutions of the labour movement were built and are still, after so many changes, most evident. Or take another example which I usually irritate my friends by mentioning. The General Strike of 1926 was a high-point of working-class self-organisation and protest. It was strong in many places and indeed present and active in most. But look also at that less convenient memory of 1926: at that organisation for strike-breaking against the organised working class: the OMS, the Organisation for the Maintenance of Supplies, one of those things we've half-forgotten although may we see its like again. Look where that was recruited. It was not, as some of the books tell you, all undergraduates and their debutante friends. It really was not.

In certain parts of the country where the problems of social self-definition, of class consciousness in that hard, arresting, challenging form are in fact quite different, there was significant recruiting of poor men against what was objectively their own class. For those were the mixed communities where the labour processes do not deliver with them a community which gives you a common identity from the beginning; where you can be simultaneously a local patriot, a loyal member of the working class, a good neighbour, a good member of the family; it is all one or nearly one. Get to a mixed community, get to where people are living next door to each other but are not necessarily in the same kind of work, get to where there are radical differences of social situation and position right inside the community and you have a different basic sense of what a community is.

It is then no surprise at all that most of the positive working-class novels have been written from inside the self-conscious and confident working-class communities. What is a surprise is that the first socialist working-class novel in English was written in the other kind of place: in a community which did not, so to say, deliver class consciousness, but actually obstructed and confused it. And then of course we see what we should have seen before: that this is the key to *The Ragged-Arsed Philanthropists*. It is this that determines much of the actual strategy and tone of the book.

The novel is as it is because what Tressell is writing about is a place which is not at all like those archetypal working-class communities. It is not a place where, although there are local representatives of the employing class such as the local managers, foremen and so on and sometimes in those stages even a few proprietors, the dominant definition of 'local people' is a working class already organised by a single or one major labour process. In those close communities it is all positive; everybody is working class. This gives a marvellous integrity to the novels, but where is anyone else? You're fighting against something which you call the system, but actualizing it inside this warm community life is often very difficult, except in arguments among yourselves. In the other sort of community – as Hastings, Mugsborough, was and is – with a few mixed trades, with people working for the corporation, people working in the public utilities, people working on the railway and on the buses, in shops and hotels, and of course the building craftsmen, trademen, labourers, it feels very different. There is no common overriding loyalty proceeding from the conditions of the mining village or dockyard street – nothing like that. There is then a problem of self-perception among working men from the beginning. And beyond that, as you can see in the character of most of the trades, you have not major production for a general market but precisely, in majority, service jobs for a mixed community in which the ultimate employers are people in a different social situation on whom you depend for getting any custom and trade at all. Moreover the intermediaries, typically the small employers, the local shop-owners, building-firm owners, or even the Council that Tressell so memorably shows, these are not the big capitalist employers, who by that stage of the early twentieth century in Britain as a whole were the dominant people, and against them in those other areas self-conscious movements were formed and forming and, although it was never unified, a certain collectivity was given.

What Tressell faced in Mugsborough was this very different situation, in some ways a much harder situation. People from those relatively uniform, working-class communities often speak with a quite unreasonable kind of patronage about working-class organisations in less developed or more backward parts of the society. They often fail to realise how much of their own consciousness comes wrapped in the much more available facts of neighbourhood, work-place and local loyalty. Once you get into the mixed community, and in particular one which is relying on people bringing money in from outside as tourists or residents, then the argument about trade, about wages, about whom you are dependent on, about how you should conduct yourself as a working man, where your money comes from, what the future of the country has to be, what makes common sense – that is transformed. To argue the socialist case in that kind of community is a much harder job. Yet the remarkable fact remains that this first successful working-class novel was generated in those circumstances and not from inside the working class in the more settled and conscious communities.

Of course this has an effect on its strategies. I think we have to say two things at once about Tressell's position as a writer: two things at once (there's no way of saying it, but although I say them one after the other they are both aspects of a single statement). One, that he was writing his novel while he was a worker fully engaged in his own work. It is in that sense authentically a novel from inside the working class, very different from many examples before and after it. The working-class situation is entirely contemporary with the writing, not from an earlier time, a memory or a reconstruction. It is directly from a man who comes home from his job, writes, goes back to his job, writes, all under pressure. But second, *and at the same time,* he is for quite evident reasons, at some level of his mind – and it's very important to him – an outsider, a man in certain respects very conscious of *difference*. I mean not only that he comes from elsewhere, with his Liverpool and Irish connections; that he'd been in South Africa, in a much more complex, harder fought, colonial culture; that he'd come back and eventually ended in a seaside resort where the very fact that he'd travelled that much, that he'd seen that much of the world, gave him from the beginning a different perspective. I mean also what it was very important to know, as the biography was eventually assembled, that this was in many ways a very literate man; that his command of languages was very wide; that he was a man capable of sustained reading and of assessing statistics. And then there was this double situation, that he was coming home day by day, from hard slog to earn his bread, doing his job and yet with a mind which had reached a different perspective, having read and having seen other parts of the world. So he knew that a familiar kind of deference, an acceptance of the formula that to live you have to get favour from the ones with money or custom that offer it, wasn't an immutable law of life but a specific social condition. He also knew from his reading that the arguments so proudly produced by supposedly educated people that the economic situation was inevitably like this were usually quite shallow, and that many of those who looked down on labouring men were themselves very ignorant in terms of conventional education and knowledge.

Then, from this double vision, the bitter irony of the title – *Ragged-Arsed* and *Philanthropists* – is the best way of reminding us that the book has advantages which the most positive, realist novels from inside working-class communities don't usually have. It also (inevitably because it has other things to do) has less of the sustained substance of that other fiction at its best. Actually, it is very difficult to assess the proportions of the different modes. In actual length most of the book does after all follow individuals and families, follow them through typical crises: of death, of seduction, of betrayal; of illness and accidents; and through and beyond these the affections of family life. In the other kind of working-class novel such feelings extend outwards, from kindness to neighbours to loyalty to mates to loyalty to the union to loyalty to socialism, without too many barriers being set up because it's much the same feeling being a neighbour and defining yourself collectively as this kind of industrial and political person. Among the ragged-arsed inhabitants of that deliberately named Mugsborough, the structure of feeling is very different and there is a bitterness which could only have been let out in any tolerable way by a man who was also earing his bread directly as a working man.

Indeed there are parts of this book which, taken on their own – which is quite wrong to do, but analytically you can hypothesize it – have such savage things to say about so many working-class people, about the general conditions of ignorance and misunderstanding and cruelty, that there is hardly a line between them and a certain kind of reactionary rendering of the working class and working people as irredeemably incapable of improving their conditions. Tressell's awareness of this is beautifully dramatised in Barrington's encounter with the renegade who is able to say: 'You have these wonderful ideas for the future of the class and for the future of society. I know these people. I know what they're like, I know how they think, and I know you're wasting your time'. [paraphrase, **pp 584-7**, pp 541-4]

This is the kind of position which becomes a problem again in a writer like Orwell who typically did not include in his diaries or notebooks those working-class men and women he met who were well-read, articulate, politically conscious or active in some pursuit which is conventionally not assigned to the class. If, on the other hand, he met somebody who fitted a middle-class vision of the drunken or feckless or ignorant or helpless working man, down it went. When he wrote *The Road to Wigan Pier* he sought out the lowest doss-house in town, even though he'd arrived with introductions from leaders of the Unemployed Workers' Movement and trade unionists and had stayed with educated working-class socialists. He then 'proved' that socialism is just a middle-class idea. Working-class people are either just not interested or they've got more common sense or they're good-natured, thoughtless, rather childish and at times drunken people – what he represented in *Nineteen Eighty-Four* as the Proles.

Now, something not too far from that is often very near the edge in Tressell precisely because the whole inner tension of the book at once an entire and, at that level, almost involuntary commitment which comes from going back day after day to that kind of exploiting job, and a special concern which quickly becomes anger, rage even, despair often, at the fact that people will not admit their common condition, that they will accept any phoney explanation or distraction, that they will listen to their actual exploiters and believe the most self-evident rubbish rather than admit the truth of their own lives. The rarest and most invigorating quality of Tressell is that he goes head down, head up at that kind of ignominy which could only ever be challenged effectively, could indeed only ever be represented effectively, from inside. It's been done repeatedly from outside, but then it always goes sour. In Tressell it is a fresh, clean anger. Moreover it is at once put into tension with what is *nevertheless* (and that word should be emphasized) an absolute belief that conditions can be changed, that they can be changed by this class, that what is described by others as a mere ideal is perfectly available and practicable, and that it really doesn't depend on the assumption, typically complained about, that people are more unselfish, more noble than they are.

The argument is precisely challenged at that point, for socialism is not really to do with that. It is to do with understanding social relations, understanding the system. If experience alone will not teach, then experience *and teaching* will teach. That kind of confidence is decisive although it doesn't come easily. Great care is taken to show something very different from the easy ideas of bringing the truth, bringing the message and being gratefully received by the suffering masses. On the contrary, we see Owen being beaten up, we see things which are like the reception of the nineteenth-century Russian populists who went out and told the peasants that they were poor and ignorant and that they'd come to educate them, and who were sometimes lucky to escape the village alive. This is the whole experience of coming even with the truth to people already so hard-pressed that truth is a short-term question, if it's a question at all. In Tressell this happens from inside and is seen both ways. But not as an evasion, for he includes – it is the most radical innovation in this work, often sitting uneasily with the other writing but there it is, extraordinarily successful – the two interventions which do what to this day the fiction text-books tell you you can't do. I mean the two teaching chapters, 'The Oblong' and 'The Great Oration'.

In 'The Oblong' you get a figurative demonstration of an analysis of the social order which leads to certain clear conclusions about it. It is given by a man to whom we've been introduced in a rounded, fictional way for people whom we've got to know in rather more angry ways but nevertheless whom we know as people and as names. It is just done; it is not apologetically done. It's done as demonstration, characteristically in the form of a visual figure – Tressell as Noonan the signwriter. 'The Great Oration' is the inclusion, with remarkable courage as a writer, not only of a long speech about the new socialist order – a speech full of some difficult socialist positions of that time, through mainly a typical early-twentieth-century form of state socialism, with the notion of the industrial army. It is the inclusion of the full speech, and at the same time of the reactions and interactions. The chairman, the interrupters and the general scene reproduce just that consciousness which is resistant to sustained, serious talk, and this is not for light relief; indeed it shows both the need and the problem of that kind of serious discourse.

So there is this innovation of inserting (it would now be done more often in avant-garde fiction) levels of discourse which do not cancel each other, and both teaching and the problems of teaching are there. It is done because experience alone will not teach, as in a way it does or is supposed to do in the positive kind of working-class novel – 'You've seen people suffering; you've seen them suffering undeservedly; you say people should not live like this; let them – even, at times, let us – not live like this'. That is what that kind of novel typically offers. And yet, reproducing itself from generation to generation, even with marginal improvements often of a significant kind, that *general* condition persists. What Tressell has tackled is not just the pity of it, which recommends sympathy, which passes too easily into the notion that we could all live better and differently if we'd only make up our minds to. The book gets to that position in the end, but it halts very deliberately along the way to see what is really involved in making up your mind about it, setting your mind to it. It looks hard at the obstacles, the barriers which are put up not only among those who have a lot to lose but among those who have everything to gain. That is the savage sense and that's why we have to say *The Ragged-Arsed Philanthropists*, with its much harsher edge. That is what is being said: these are people whose own conditions ought to force them into consciousness, who are nevertheless engaged in the large-scale philanthropy of subsidising people who either do not work at all or work much less hard and for much more reward than the journeymen and labourers.

This hard, satiric tone goes back to a different tradition from that of the realist novel. It goes back, in quite an immediate sense, to Cobbett. In the early nineteenth century, that great representative figure of the common people of England said, harshly: 'I despise a poor man who is contented'. This rejects the arguments, usually of the rich, that you can be contented even if poor or the other kind of argument that, although poor in material goods, although lacking social status or respect, nevertheless we're good people. This harsher tone from Cobbett rejects that absolutely. He says, in effect: to be poor and contented is below the quality of man. To be deprived and cheated and yet still to be contented is below the quality of a man. It is to lack self-respect.

This is then generalised from an individual to a class. If a body of people are suffering conditions they ought not to suffer, conditions which are avoidable, and yet they somehow find reasons for contentment or even acquiescence and co-operation with what is making them like that, then no kind words. An ultimate sympathy is there but its tone is harsh. As Owen thinks in his worst moments, the real enemy, the real oppressors, are the people who soak in the daily evidence of their condition and yet remain content; who displace their dissatisfaction onto other people; who refuse with extraordinary complacency any talk which would try to explain their condition. In the book as a whole, the conditions for sympathy are created and then cut across by something so sharp and challenging that it could only come from that double situation of the writer, inside and outside: inside the condition of the class, outside its consciousness.

We can then go back further, to quite a different tradition, to Bunyan. As you read in Tressell the description of the Mugsborough Organized Benevolence Society and those who were present, you can hear the tradition, a popular tradition, which gets printed in Bunyan but which is much older than him:

> The Mayor, Alderman Sweater, presided, and amongst those present were Sir Graball D'Encloseland, Lady D'Encloseland, Lady Slumrent, Rev. Mr. Bosher, Mr. Cheeseman, Mrs. Bilder,

> Mrs. Grosare, Mrs. Daree, Mrs. Butcher, Mrs. Taylor, Mrs. Baker, Mrs. Starvem.... [**p 368**, p 339]

and there follows about a quarter of a column of names of other charitable persons. That is the Bunyan tactic of attaching at once the names of social positions and the names of moral qualities or their absence. It is an assembly of the respectable who are on their way to damnation. Or at least Bunyan could have said that. The great confidence of *that* popular and radical tradition was that the wicked of the world were on their way to hell, and that the virtuous Christian could name them by the names God should have given them and would give them when it came to judgement, while Christian himself had his own pilgrimage.

For a socialist writer in the same tradition it is not so clear. There is historical optimism but it is less close than that kind of Christian perspective. You can say that Noonan-Tressell, like the other socialists he described, a small minority among building workers – and other workers – belongs to a vanguard. It's a very honourable, heroic thing to be in the vanguard of a great cause. It's also of course a standing temptation to pride that all around you is ignorance, wilful ignorance, an inability to understand, but you hold your place, you continue the work. It is for this reason that Tressell has always appealed especially to relatively isolated militants and questioning men. Pride either way: a justified pride or at times that angry pride that controls isolation and depression. In Tressell the full justification comes through,not only because it is done from inside but because he sees so clearly, beyond the heroics and the anger, that such men are themselves going to be crushed down. When Owen starts coughing blood, and beyond the general condition there is this suffering but still clear-sighted man, we are shown that double condition of hero and victim, neither acknowledged by others, which is a true inner history of so long and so hard a cause.

Tressell needed if only for that reason the figure of Barrington, the wealthy young man who takes up labouring work in a kind of benevolence, to find out the conditions of working people, to experience them directly, yet in the end can withdraw from them, use his own money for the comfort of the Christmas presents or, as in that episode near the end, go away and come back to finance the socialist van. That kind of wealthy young sympathiser, participator, has his own crisis of confidence as he encounters not only the conditions but the ignorance and the refusals. Yet it is less bitter than Owen who is inside it, where the bitterness is not just that they won't see the light, which is an abstract way of putting the problem, but that if they go on being this stupid, 'what sort of world are my children going to grow up in?' That's hard. That's not just saying, 'Wait, for the time is coming when the campaign will succeed'. It's saying, 'Is there going to be a world for my kids if people go on being this stupid?' It's a hard question and it's put hard and it should be taken hard.

There is another question, finally, which must continually have occupied Tressell. It's a problem anyway for a man of his varied history, from Liverpool and then from South Africa, coming to a smallish, southern English provincial town. It is the problem of the level of working-class literacy and its relation to working class speech. I was very interested in that chapter in Fred Ball's book about restoring the manuscript; about the inconsistencies of spelling, the problems of grammar, the problems of abbreviations, the general problems of the representation of working-class speech.

Now first there is no finer representation, anywhere in English writing, of a certain rough-edged, mocking, give-and-take conversation between workmen and mates. This humour, this edge, is one of the most remarkable achievements. But he was interested also in something else which relates to the wider theme. It was obviously a very sore point, to a man earning his living with his hands who knew himself to be a man of substantial intelligence and mental accomplishment, that the standard response to working men who talked about socialism or how the country should be run differently was to say that they were ignorant. So he took great care with the Brigands – the people who ran the town council, the small employers, the Forty Thieves as I heard somebody in Hastings, when I was living here, say we still ought to call them – I make no comment on that – he took great care to show the Brigands as ignorant people. He uses all the devices of what I have called the orthography of the uneducated, all that torturing of the already tortured nature of English spelling, to indicate that somebody's pronunciation is not standard, not educated. This always leads to the most extraordinary contortions since, if you believe that English sounds are represented by English spelling, so that there is a standard from which some 'dialect' divergence can be identified by a spelling divergence, then you get into this curious situation in which it is really different in a novel for somebody to say 'I love you' spelled I l-o-v-e y-o-u and to say 'I love you' spelled I l-u-v y-e-r. But different in what sense? We are asked to take the first seriously or at least to wait and see how it works out. The second is marked for a different response. What sort of emotion is that – 'I luv yer'? Probably very vulgar and inadequate. You are represented as feeling or thinking through your spelling, although of course you're not spelling anyway – the writer is spelling – you're just talking in the language of your own place.

Now, Tressell uses this for the Brigands to show that, although they are puffing themselves up, they are in fact ignorant people. But he uses it also in a kind of counterpoint between people who have got some sense and people who haven't. It's a very interesting differentiation, not in class terms but as a literary technique. Compare, for example, the way Owen and his family speak to each other, usually in standard orthography, and the way the men speak to each other at work, in ways carefully indicated by the distorted spelling.

There's a marvellous example in 'The Great Oration':

> "And there's another thing I objects to," said Crass. "And that's all this 'ere talk about hignorance: wot about all the money wots spent every year for edication?"

The one word I would especially bring to your attention, because it's symbolic of this whole larger problem, is 'Wot': "Wot about all the money...." – w-o-t.

> "You should rather say – [Barrington replies] 'What about all the money that's wasted every year on education?' " **[p 514,** p 474]

W-h-a-t. Now since everyone knows that somebody who is represented in the text as saying w-o-t is ignorant, can we invite any native English speaker to pronounce the word spelled w-h-a-t in a way that is not w-o-t? I mean try it. In fact everyone says w-o-t, but this is a device for distinction between someone who knows what he is talking about, and for him you spell w-h-a-t, and for somebody who doesn't know what he's talking about and for him you spell w-o-t.

This kind of contrast is entwined with the challenge of the book. It is part of a textual strategy which is not necessarily entirely conscious but which is so regular that it can't be accidental. It is in one sense repeating a standard prejudice of English middle-class writing, but within a broader strategy which is the whole point of the book. For he is saying that it is terrible for people to have to live like this when they are doing useful and good work, and could do more useful and better work in different circumstances. It is terrible to live like this, to be this vulnerable to the whims of others, to be this vulnerable to the accidents of trade and the imbecilities of the system. It is terrible also, however, to be vulnerable not only to propaganda and the self-justifications of others who have an interest in perpetuating ignorance, but to an ignorance that gets built in, inside people themselves – an ignorance that becomes their common sense. Being a prisoner can come to seem common sense, or can be made to seem what it is to be human. There is one way of responding to this, by pitying the person, as in certain parts of the novel Tressell does.

But there is also another way, still an original and a lasting way. And that is to say: 'You are a prisoner, and you'll only get out of this prison if you'll admit it's a prison. And if you won't call it a prison, I will, and I'll go on calling it a prison come what may.' This strength, this challenge, is the lasting quality of Tressell's book, *The Ragged-Arsed Philanthropists*!

Tressell and the Unions

Norman Willis

16 April 1984, White Rock Pavilion, Hastings

I am proud to give the Robert Tressell lecture. One of the great statements about lecturers comes from Joe Philpot who says: "It's no use booin' and threatenin', because 'e's one of them lecturers wot can honly be managed with kindness." [**p 280,** p 259]. *The Ragged Trousered Philanthropists* is, as has been said many times, one of the most influential books of the British labour movement. I suppose that it's made more socialists than any piece of literature in the English language and certainly sustained and developed people's beliefs in the campaigns that they've undertaken.

I remember going up to Liverpool in 1977 when John Nettleton organised the laying of the stone over Robert Noonan's grave, and because of some complications I flew to Manchester from Heathrow and was driven to Heathrow by a rather elderly chap in a car. We got into conversation about current affairs and he told me that he was a Tory voter. He said, "I've been a poor man all my life but I've always believed that you should vote for rich businessmen because they know how to run things." It seemed to me to be peculiarly appropriate that some sixty years or so after the book was written, there was a statement made that could have come from almost any page in *The Ragged Trousered Philanthropists*.

I first came into contact with the book as a play at the Unity Theatre. When someone earlier on mentioned it, I misheard and thought that the title of the book was 'The Ragged Trousered *Philosophers*' because (and it shows why the book needed to be written) the romantic concept, of poverty turning people into action, people made wise and philosophic by their working-class experience, made eloquent by injustices and their needs, was a very obvious part of the socialist and working-class literary tradition. But Robert Noonan turned all that on its head. He showed the tension between someone advocating a very clear view and people who had not been made eloquent by injustice, but numbed by their experiences. Noonan turned first of all to the situation as he saw it and then to the solution, not only through moral revulsion from what he saw but also very much from the history of many parts of socialist literature criticising the inefficiency of the class system. Earlier in the book comes something which relates, it seems to me, directly to things that have happened since and are happening now:

> These are the 'practical' men; the monopolists of intelligence, the wise individuals who control the affairs of the world: it is in accordance with the ideas of such men as these that the conditions of human life are regulated.
>
> This is the position:
>
> It is admitted that never before in the history of mankind was it possible to produce the necessaries of life in such abundance as at present.
>
> The management of the affairs of the world – the business of arranging the conditions under which we live – is at present in the hands of Practical, Level-headed, Sensible Business-men.
>
> The result of their management is, that the majority of the people find it a hard struggle to live. Large numbers exist in perpetual poverty: a great many more periodically starve: many actually die of want: hundreds destroy themselves rather than continue to live and suffer.
>
> When the Practical, Level-headed, Sensible Business-men are asked why they do not remedy this state of things, they reply that they do not know what to do! or, that it is impossible to remedy it! [**pp 377-8**, pp 347-8]

That sounds almost like saying 'there is no alternative'. All the people willing to work, clamouring to be allowed to, but the practical, level-head, sensible businessmen did not know what to do.

Consider where we still are with the continued rule of these people: the great sewerage systems are falling to bits, hundreds of thousands of people are still homeless and many more are living in houses that are falling to bits, hundreds of thousands of building workers, people with the same skills that are shown in the book, are not being allowed to build, and educational provision is being cut. We should look, beyond the boundaries of this country, at the poverty that has not been solved by the present sort of sensible, business arithmetic. We still have to make the case for *our* sort of sensible arithmetic that is based upon community care, the sharing of responsibility, the sharing of resources and the fact that most of the problems that now confront the great mass of working people in this country cannot be solved, and will not be solved, by the arithmetic of the market forces that are displayed in full ferocity in *The Ragged Trousered Philanthropists*. Robert Noonan, through Owen, described it as an 'insane, idiotic, imbecile system'. [**p 286**, p 265] But the simple fact is that we still have to make that case and we still have to make the connections that, in part, are made in Noonan's book.

There are many ways in which the book is a product of its time: the vein of teetotalism, the underlying references to prostitution (although it is not a book that deals directly with the problems of the women's movement as such), and the argument about the role of money – great scenes when, against enormous cheers and jeers, Owen seeks to establish that the problem is not shortage of money, which many of his fellows can't understand because they *are* short of money and believe, as long as you get a bit more, it solves the problem, but the issue of wealth and the issue of resources.

There are ways in which Tressell's book could run into conflict with some people in the trade union movement. There are many people in affiliated unions now, who wouldn't necessarily accept that insurance agents, shop assistants or clerks were to be classified as doing '*unnecessary* work'. [**p 289**, p 268] But what is of direct relevance is the way in which the men who work in the Cave (the house that's being decorated) are subject to fear, arising from the fact that they were unprotected by organisation or legislation of any kind, and the way in which, as the seasons change, this directly affects their lives as much as if they were prehistoric cavemen.

Moral criticism also comes through the book, which is another great strain in socialist working-class literature and campaigning. Tressell shows the intimate link between the quality of the work that they did and the man who gets sacked because he is taking too long; the way scamping of work puts people out of work – a job which was scheduled for four months is done in nine weeks , "and now", as one of the workers says, "now we can all go to hell". Not only at the time that they were unemployed was this fear with them but the fact that they knew that it was ever present; the scenes throughout the book where, on different Saturdays, they were astonished, relieved and surprised that they were not all laid off. And, as one of the delegates at the conference said, "However many creeping points they've got, no-one is immune." Tressell quotes from a song which has one of the most beautiful tunes and some of the greatest lines, *England Arise* – "Out of your evil dream of toil and sorrow." And that was exactly what it was, always the fear, always the inability to be able to look further ahead than today because if you got through today that was just good enough.

I think that one of the historic difficulties, and indeed one of the historic weaknesses, of the British working-class movement also comes through in Noonan's descriptions. There's the people who talk about free trade, there's the people who are Liberals, the people who are Tories, and all the argument that goes on, a lot of it focusing on the very articulate case that Owen not only puts, but in a way isolates him in the discussion (that I think Noonan wanted to show). But one of the weaknesses that comes through is that whilst there is a reference to the Society, the painters' union, the immediate necessity to stand together, although put in general, doesn't emerge as an immediate objective. It's hard for anyone who's never experienced these things to say, but when you look at some of the redundancy issues seventy years later (I don't say they're all like this, but unfortunately in the last few years far too many of them have had these sorts of overtones), far too many of them have produced exactly the same sort of arguments. But the need to build an organisation at the point of work, which may sometimes be defeated but has frequently been successful with great pioneering sacrifice, that never emerges as the issue.

The Ragged Trousered Philanthropists is about the human situation that is created by circumstances in which people live in immediate fear and are often reluctant, in fact very antagonistic towards the idea of controlling their own lives, their own destinies. I have no great rosy spectacles to look through at the trade union movement – I like it too much to be romantic about it – but in these circumstances, at its best (and it often is at its best) you can learn, you can control and you can start to do something about it. James Connolly wrote these words about the trade union movement: 'The Union found the workers on their knees and strove to raise them to the erect position of manhood' (and I think we would now include womanhood very much directly in that, but this is what he said). Then, importantly, he said:

> It found them with all the vices of slavery in their souls and has striven to eradicate these vices and replace them with the virtues of free people. It found them with no other weapons of defence than the arts of the liar, the lickspittle and the toady and it combined them and taught them to abhor those arts and to rely proudly on the defensive power of combination.

Now that is saying something about whether you can live from day to day. It makes a moral case for collective combination, which doesn't mean that you turn round and say that it's all perfect. On the contrary, if that opportunity is open to us, then we have a duty to make trade unions as good as that says; not to say that there is nothing wrong with them or that by some instinct they will always do the right thing – they do too many things for it ever to be possible they get it right every time. People turn to collective action out of an instinct that they will get a better deal and have a better future and, I believe, in many respects be better individuals through it. And it doesn't matter how much the pressure is against you, whether it's in Poland or South Africa or wherever. Some people take to this because of a political belief, some because they've read something or been contacted by a union. But in many of the most decisive battles of the British trade union movement, they didn't need that; they needed an instinct that they had to stand together as people.

When we're told that in those days we were taught to work jolly hard and that the puritan and Victorian values have to be returned to, then those sorts of statements are not only, I believe, an insult to the unemployed, they're an insult probably to the puritans and certainly to the Victorians. First of all, you didn't have to put up with it. It wasn't natural that people should be unemployed, it wasn't natural that there should be a hierarchy; it wasn't natural that there should be constant poverty. There was no natural order that said that certain people should have a great deal and many other people nothing at all. It was something that had to be overcome and could be overcome. Second point: the history and day-to-day experience of a lot of working people had told them that it needed collective action that, increasingly as the years went by, expressed itself in terms of community action through the state. Coming through was the idea there were solutions and those solutions lay in our own hands and they were collective.

Unions are now carrying on a campaign against privatisation. Public ownership and a degree of state action, for a very long period, was not contested because there didn't seem to be enough money to pull it back. I don't believe that the present campaign for privatisation actually started simply with money; it was just an offence to the concept that private interest and private individuals had to control things. Noonan deals with the same problem in his book.

Although it's now about great individuals, great entrepreneurs, making money, and that's what made Britain great and able to carry on more savage wars than they've been able to do before, one of the prime things was the fact that services and the concept of public service started to be developed, whether it was in education, state administration, public transport or the postal service (a great element of freedom which meant that you could start to develop communications throughout the country that were vital to the development of a democratic society and a democratic trade union movement). We are now facing a reduction in the post office service, which is not just an issue of employment in the industry, important though it is, but also an issue about freedom, and particularly for elderly people. The same thing applies to public transport, housing and, of course, perhaps most dramatically, the National Health Service.

All that was built up, so don't let us pretend that these people weren't good enough to become bosses, or didn't have the skills. Some did. Indeed the main character in this book, Owen, was himself a very skilled man. When he's given the chance to do the Moorish decorations in one of the rooms, although he understands the system, the exploitation, and gives the economic and political analysis of why people are forced to work too long and too hard, Owen still can't avoid the temptation of doing extra work himself because he wants the chance to use his skills. So he promises that he will work at home, get his own cartridge paper to draw on and get spare wallpaper. He comes alive as an individual when he is kept on at work for that reason. Later on, when he's trying to get work, he's ashamed of himself when he realises that he's saying, 'Take your work away from the other man and employ me'. And, with all the difficulties, he makes a stand on behalf of the young apprentice, first of all demanding that the boy be given what was contracted to him, which had never been given to him, the chance to be trained, but also the chance to be human.

The ones who are jeering at Owen, the ones who are giving simplistic explanations, the ones who like a good talk but believe that there is something alien about it, at the same time I don't think that the book says they are beyond hope. What it does is to describe the circumstances in which they become the ragged trousered philanthropists and their own worst enemy.

And so the first point I want to make about the book and the circumstances it describes is that the relation between the concept of collective, caring, community state action, socialism, democratic socialism (call it what you may) on the one hand, and the day-to-day protection and work of trade unionism on the other hand, is one that if we don't make it will mean that both groups (if they are groups, and they're frequently not separate people) will suffer. I think they're a mirror image of each other and that without that connection both socialism and trade unionism suffer.

I believe that that lesson has to be drawn, that it's not necessary to tell the people all the time they have to be socialists or trade unionists, that they've got to attend a lecture or got to accept every dot and comma of every policy that's put forward. Certainly we need to make the case that it will always be true that the community has to look after itself because individuals are not going to do it. There were great charitable people in the nineteenth century, there are great charitable people now, and some people will receive something directly from that (and I make no criticisms of them for being that; rather they were that way than anything else). But that does not produce a solution for our hospitals, it doesn't produce a solution for our schools, it doesn't produce a solution for our roads or our houses. What we have to do is to get that collective thing and make it good.

The trade union movement, it seems to me, faces enormous dilemmas about the future. Some say forecasting is very difficult, others say 'Why should we worry about posterity, what the hell did posterity ever do for us?' But the truth is that posterity and the future starts the second after you've said it. I believe that, given the situation that has emerged, produced and encouraged by exactly the same sort of mismanagement that is described in *The Ragged Trousered*

Philanthropists, the trade union movement has to develop and make its priorities in areas which will sometimes be at the particular point of work and sometimes seem to be a long way away in solutions.

Primarily, of course, that relates to the problem of unemployment. Unemployment is not only vicious in itself, it is one of the great underminers of collective action in the trade union movement, and the government knows it. Because of the economic fallacies they pursue, it has followed that policy for that reason. Some people have developed skills which have been rewarded in our society. Others have developed equal skills, often related to community service, such as in the health service, but are not rewarded in the same way. The compassion and the service given by people in those circumstances is played upon and taken advantage of, not only by the government but by many other substantial parts of the community.

I believe we have to restate again two things: one, that we have moral, political and economic objections to unemployment; and second, to say again, it need not be, there are many things that can, must be done about it. For example, the People's March which starts next Saturday is not just a protest, but a moving, self-educating force. In 1932 Baldwin said, "If the people cannot cure unemployment, the government cannot cure it for them". That is back again and has to be answered passionately.

Anything I've said here, about the misuse of resources, lack of collective control, lack of community care, can be written a thousandfold if you move outside this country and you think of the world as a whole – that with all the sophistication we've now got, all the economic analysis, all the means of communication, all these people who can destroy the world can't bring it together and can't reach agreement about one single, major, basic economic policy for the future of the world, except to make it worse.

So we have to find a way through. As they've found out in what I believe are politely called 'centrally controlled economies', you can't do it from the top and neither can you do it just by discussion. You actually have to have collective decision-making, collective experience. Listening to people helps; very often a lot of interesting points come up. There is the story about the man in the 1930s who went to a lecture on how to make a nourishing stew of cods heads and at the end the lady said, "Any questions?" The man put his hand up and asked, "Who's getting the rest of the cod?" That is also a question we have to ask, one that is often difficult for people now to respond to. We have had immense difficulty in arguing about pension funds. We have had more conferences about pension funds now than certainly they ever had hot dinners, and we're starting to make the case that this is workers' money that then gets outside their control, and they have to have a part in it and, indeed, since this is now a much bigger area of investment than the area of private investment, we now want to see that that goes into producing jobs, to giving back to the working community what has been taken off them. And we still have to have that argument.

I've been accused (not that I'm bothered that much) that in the class war I was only fit to be a hostage. Well, perhaps. And I'll tell you why that was said. My argument with them was this; that out of some of the situations which are inherent and some of the situations which we develop, you have to take people with you. There's not much point being right in isolation. Of course, you've got to be right, but you have to develop and time is against us. The quotation that I used then was one from a well known Renfrewshire philosopher in the seventeenth century who said, "It is better by far to be within one Scots mile of where you are making for than exactly on the spot of somewhere else". It means that you've got to develop your policies.

The trade union movement has been forced to politicise the discussion and to politicise ourselves because of the very specific attacks being made. People came to realise some of the things that they were losing: a telephone kiosk may not be the biggest thing to lose in the world, unless you want to make a call and you haven't got a phone; a bus may not be that important unless you want to go somewhere and, like many in rural areas and many older people, you've got no other means of transport; and, without going into life and death in the health services, the simple fact that, seventy years after *The Ragged Trousered Philanthropists* was written, it is still true that a child born to parents where the wage-earner is unskilled has a lesser chance of surviving, of living, than someone born into the family of a bank manager or a rich person. I'm not saying, of course, that progress hasn't been made – we should be ashamed of ourselves if we hadn't – but it does mean that these things have to be fought for, that basic economic and political analysis has to be made.

What Tressell was saying was that many people ceased to live, in the fullest sense of the word, when they arrived at work. You meet too many people who for some reason believe that things like the arts or environmental issues can't be pursued through the trade union movement, some sort of macho idea that that is not our concern. If we listened to our own people, if we did the analysis, if we put the two things together, we would find that many of our people are saying to us very different things than we believe they're saying or what we are told they're saying.

A slightly more light-hearted man perhaps than Robert Noonan, Claude Coburn, once said that socialism might not be the way of getting us into heaven, but it sure was the only way of staying out of hell. Now I'm a bit glib about that: I'm not every minute in hell or things like that

– it denigrates our case to say so. But too much of what is in Noonan's book still exists, given the time that we've had and on occasion the power we've had. Some of that exists – and it's not the case that the leader has always betrayed us; I believe it is often the way that we work, and there are leaders at all sorts of levels. There are great and hopeful things in the British socialist movement and in the British trade union movement.

I believe that we have to learn these lessons in the *The Ragged Trousered Philanthropists*, and also give emphasis to some of the things that don't emerge with quite the same crystal clarity there, and operate them and do them. Two very brief final points; one, time is not on our side. Secondly, I believe that we can succeed.

Robert Tressell's Message for Today

Jack Jones

10 March 1984, Falaise Hall, Hastings

First of all, I'd like to say how pleased I am to be here and to pay tribute to the author of *The Ragged Trousered Philanthropists*. You'll remember that Robert Noonan – that was his real name, not Robert Tressell – worked here in Hastings as a painter and his book describes the work of the building trade in the early part of the century. Looking round Hastings I'm bound to say that if Robert Noonan was alive today he and his colleagues, the painters, would have plenty of work to do, and I can tell you that in London, where I live, painters and architects and builders would have an enormous amount of work to do if only they would be allowed to do it. It's amazing to me to see the enormous amount of work to be done to rehabilitate our buildings and our housing and generally the living conditions of the people, and at the same time to know that we have got nearly four million unemployed. There must be something wrong that we should have this difference between masses of unemployed anxious to work on the one side and lots of work to be done to make our lives better, and somehow we can't seem to resolve that problem. And that's in a sense what Robert Noonan sought to describe and in a way to find the answer to.

I first read the book when I was a young apprentice in Liverpool, the city in which Robert Noonan died, and it had a profound impression on me. It also had a profound impression on many, many workmen in my time when I was an apprentice and since. Noonan, incidentally, was buried in a paupers' grave in Liverpool. I was present when we unveiled a huge stone over it and there were twelve names on the gravestone, all of them paupers. Robert Noonan's name was there and of course the purpose of the gravestone was to recognise the contribution he had made. But those who had been buried with him also had their names engraved on the stone, a reflection of those bitter times.

Without question and without doubt, his message still has relevance today and one who has contributed greatly to making sure that that message is still carried forward is here, Fred Ball of Hastings who discovered the unabridged text of the book written by Tressell, in working man's handwriting and working man's language. It wasn't published as a fully unabridged edition until Fred Ball made sure that it was published, and there's been an enormous interest since that time. It's been published, I believe, in Japanese for example.

All over the world there's a great deal of interest because there's no doubt the book itself is written in such a way that the ordinary person can understand clearly what it's all about. And I'd like to pay tribute to Fred Ball and the Workers' Educational Association and indeed all those concerned here in Hastings with bringing the attention of large numbers of people to *The Ragged Trousered Philanthropists* because through their efforts socialism has become a more active factor in the thinking of people.

The book not only exposes the hypocrisy and hollowness of Victorian and Edwardian so-called 'values', but it provides a clear-cut case for socialism, as valid now as it was when Noonan wrote it. In the words of a pamphlet that has been published under the aegis of the WEA here in Hastings:

> One of the many enduring qualities of *The Ragged Trousered Philanthropists* is its socialist vision. Robert Tressell is increasingly recognised as one of Britain's most influential socialist writers. Few have conveyed the message and hope of socialism so directly, so eloquently, so passionately and over so many years to such a wide audience. [*The Robert Tressell Papers*, p 29]

Now, despite the years that have passed, the book is still highly interesting and in my view it would be fine if all those who claim leadership in the Labour movement, and not least those who write about the movement, would read this book again and again and try to emulate the clarity of expression, the sincerity of the spirit, which animates the whole book. The exposure of exploitation of man by man shown in the Great Money Trick is a good example. The demonstration of the way in which working people were robbed by their employers, in a sense, is still valid today. I and others used to read it out and discuss it in Labour College classes in the '30s. There is need for such classes today and, believe me, Robert Noonan provided a better textbook than many of the present day academics who are now still looking apparently for what they call the 'lost millions'. They seem to think that the working class in Britain has faded away but, of course, if it had there wouldn't be much of Britain left.

Looking through the book at random, have a look at Noonan's indictment of the establishment Christians and see how reasonably on target it still is. I am particularly making this point because of the speech the other day by a man named Butcher, a Junior Minister in the Government. You will remember that he said that the job of Christian parsons was to save souls and really not bother about people, in effect. Well, there is a character in the book called Slyme, a very slimy character too he was, one of the men who sucked up to the boss on the job and would do anything to down his work-mates. He was one of those who used to preach so-called Christianity at the corner of the street. Noonan wrote:

> ...Slyme called at the Post Office to put some of his wages in the bank. Like most other 'Christians', he believed in taking thought for the morrow, what he should eat and drink and wherewithal he was to be clothed. He thought it wise to lay up for himself as much treasure upon earth as possible. The fact that Jesus said that His disciples were not to do these things made no more difference to Slyme's conduct than it does to the conduct of any other 'Christian'. They are all agreed that when Jesus said this He meant something else; and all the other inconvenient things that Jesus said are disposed of in the same way. For instance, these 'disciples' assure us that when Jesus said, 'Resist not evil', 'If a man smite thee upon the right cheek turn unto him also the left', He really meant 'Turn on to him a Maxim gun; disembowel him with a bayonet or batter in his skull with the butt end of a rifle!' When He said, 'If one take thy coat, give him thy cloak also,' the 'Christians' say that what He really meant was: 'If one take thy coat, give him six months' hard labour.' A few of the followers of Jesus admit that He really did mean just what He said, but they say that the world would never be able to go on if they followed out His teachings!

Think of those words when you see on television those establishment figures going in and out of church on a Sunday or taking part in religious ceremonies. Wouldn't it be right to say today, as Noonan wrote:

> ...why continue the hypocritical farce of calling themselves 'Christians' when they don't really believe in or follow Him at all? [**p 237**, p 220]

That's the character of the book. The book portrays the warp and weft of the lives of our fathers, the story of the working class at the turn of the century, an indictment of capitalism in words and in story as searing as any of the writings and speeches of the great socialists of all history.

But it's the criticism, in a way, of our own class that affected me most. For much of it is still true today. The ignorance, the divisions, the subservience which still stands in the way of a rapid advance to a better society, to the achievement of Robert Noonan's dreams. It's a remarkable but tragic fact that despite the enormous growth of science, of technology, of educational institutions, there is a considerable lack of comprehension amongst masses of people. In his day, William Morris wrote of the problems of the uneducated and the exploited. He said:

> The poets have sung and the builders have builded, the painters have fashioned their tales of delight, for what and for whom has the world's book been gilded, when all is for these, but the blackness of night?

How far have we advanced in the elimination of ignorance since Noonan's day? I ask the question knowing from my own experience of the inertia and lack of comprehension which prevails amongst many people. It's an alarming condition, almost as frightening in its way as the nuclear threat. If our schools were turning out a nation of reasoning, critically-minded but public-spirited citizens, well-informed on economic and political subjects and able to recognise and control their prejudices, our life would be a lot simpler. Political parties, for example, would be able to put a reasoned case before the electorate and expect to win on its merits. That's like saying if pigs could only fly. It's a reflection on all of us, our educational system, on our labour movement, that a large part of the British population remains half-educated with a narrow and self-centred outlook, a situation that's like clay in the hands of a clever, scheming, wealthy class eager to play one section of the population off against the other. It's also the core of the sick society. The chaos and the anarchy of the present day may suit those in power who find that ignorance makes easy the application of a divide-and-conquer policy. It makes possible a dictatorship of the mind by the use of the most specious propaganda with the aid of the popular media, in the main the newspapers. It may be argued that policies adopted by the present Government are desperate remedies for desperate times and that calmer weather may allow the remedies to be tested and shown to be worthy, or worthless as many of us really think they are.

The question is will the present-day leaders allow calmer weather to arrive? They are holding on to power in circumstances of massive unemployment by appearing to appease some sections of the people at the expense of others. Their policy is to divide-and-conquer and if you don't believe me you see what happens in the Budget next Tuesday. Full employment would weaken the position of our present rulers and, if it was desired, the answer is frankly easy to find; by means of sharing the work, sharing the leisure and, not least, sharing the wealth, a policy advocated by Robert Noonan in his book. But full employment facilitates a more united working class and a stronger trade union movement, and that apparently must not be permitted. So unemployment is to be dealt with not as a major problem. Other issues become front page news and divert our attention from the misery of millions without work. Minds are assaulted and battered by the press, by the radio and television, although on some issues silence, the suppression of news, is also a most effective means of misleading the public.

The history of fascism should remind us of the overwhelming effects of the ceaseless barrage of lies and suggested propaganda to which the populations of Germany, Italy and, later, Spain were exposed. The danger is that a new wave of Goebbels-type methods is beginning to spread in our country. Recent experiences have shown that penalties for lying in the press, absolute blatant lies, penalties for that are non-existent. And damn lies there have been and damn lies are still being told by sections of the press and by politicians to influence the thinking of the masses. The lie for example that pensioners in Britain are doing very well. To quote a phrase, 'they're awash with money', when in fact they are the lowest paid pensioners of all the major countries in Europe. That relieves the Chancellor from the need to make a bigger budget provision for the elderly. You look on Tuesday, he won't provide any real improvements in pensions and pensioners' conditions.

During the Falklands campaign, the normally passive British people were persuaded to become jingoistic and aggressive. For the most part they accepted any story told by the press as gospel. Some people even applauded the *Sun* when it said "Gotcha" because a ship had been sunk and large numbers of people went down – human beings. Who can doubt after the Falklands period and the recent General Election that the British media is a powerful propaganda weapon. The same no doubt could be said of the United States media treatment of the Grenada invasion. Hitler said of propaganda, "It is nothing more or less than a weapon, but a really terrible one in the hands of one who understands it" – and he did. So much propaganda is conducted through the media, especially the newspapers (I have to keep saying that because all the newspapers with the exception, I think, of the *Morning Star*, the *Guardian* and occasionally the *Daily Mirror*, are entirely in the hands of the right wing). There is no doubt that the media had a massive influence on the results in the Common Market referendum. You remember that? We started out with most of the people feeling that we shouldn't stay in, but the press persuaded people to change their minds. If they voted against the Common Market, they would lose lots of jobs; if they voted for, they would have higher wages, higher pensions and marvellous conditions! But it didn't happen!

Increasingly, because of the role of our national newspapers, the trade unions are made to appear corrupt and unpopular. If there's a little section, a minority, that disagrees with the majority, it's the minority that gets all the attention. You see what they are doing with the mining dispute at the moment. It'll be the minority that will be publicised. The little split will be exposed. But the massive unity that exists otherwise will receive little attention!

Parliament itself is brought into disrepute and endangered by the media treatment. 'Peace' becomes almost a dirty word, sex is degraded, standards are lowered to the level of the gutter, the destruction of the welfare state is encouraged, particularly the National Health Service. That has been attacked and criticised by the media to the extent that the NHS is made to appear one great big ogre rather than a great contribution to preserving the health of the nation. And, moreover, rational and reasonable discussion of issues is thrown out of the window. Even the right of reply in our press is derided, although in the United States the newspapers must publish a a reply within three days. No wonder Ernest Bevin described the newspapers of his day as the 'yellow press'. If he was alive today, he would have even more reason to use that description. Much of the propaganda tends to breed an in-built subservience amongst people, encouraging the cultivation of patronage, from touching the cap of the old days to the crawling of one level of management to another.

It's apparent even in the political field, with Members of Parliament who assume a superior and bombastic attitude outside of Parliament, but are only too ready to appease their superiors in their particular political set-up to obtain favour or advancement. That's where independence goes for a burton because the patronage of those at the top level of power is enormous in our society.

There are two types of people whose minds are especially conditioned or influenced by current propaganda. There is the pompous, self-satisfied, complacent but over-bearing person ready to support authority at all costs and often in the most aggressive manner on the one hand. The other type is the over-tolerant person who is always anxious to acquiesce or submit. The first becomes the main prop of an intolerant and and unequal society because they're usually doing well out of it. The second doesn't want to offend, prefering to keep themselves to themselves: they constitute the so-called 'silent majority', so silent they prefer not to be heard by anybody. They're the psychologically submissive; they're the people who always vote Tory because their fathers used to; they are meat and drink to the aggressive boss and the political authoritarians.

Many years ago when I was working on the docks, I remember a senior foreman who had enormous power in hiring and firing men. Unlike most of his ilk he didn't drink – very unusual – but the foremen who did drink were cultivated by the creepers in the public houses. This particular foreman, however, was religious, something like one or two of the characters in Robert Noonan's book, and I discovered that some men suddenly became church-goers. They made sure that they were seen by the foreman at the church. Others cultivated allotments and made sure that the gifts of vegetables and eggs found their way to the boss. These were the men who all too often tolerated unsafe and dangerous methods of working rather than complain. At most, they might mention the conditions surreptitiously to others like myself who were prepared to take the strain.

Well now, we've travelled a long way since those days but the old, nasty elements are still lurking about, inflamed by massive unemployment. Noonan experienced a considerable degree of subservience, and the sort of thing I've mentioned, amongst his fellow workers. Degradation, poverty, haunts the readers of the book and we are ashamed that so much indignity was suffered by members of our class.

For many there is a feeling of satisfaction that those days are finished, but are they? Some of the worst poverty in Europe is still to be found in the East End of London – and I think there is still a bit of it in Hastings too – while there are still large numbers who have to subject themselves to the means test for social security, including elderly people who have spent their lives serving the nation, to get a little bit extra to eke out the inadequate retirement pension.

The present Prime Minister justifies this Victorian outlook. Privacy independence, dignity mean little. Indeed, I was reminded of this only about ten days ago when I led a deputation of pensioners to see the Prime Minister. Her reply to the view that we should have "a respectable pension, adequate enough to live on without a means test" was that you couldn't do that: "The nation could not afford it, but of course if people were really in need they would be looked after". In her constituency, she said, "I had a lady come to me complaining that she hadn't got enough to live on. I said sit down my dear, now tell me all your circumstances." "But, Prime Minister," I said, "do you mean that you are going to do that a million times or two million times, because you've got over four million people on means-tested benefits who are pensioners? And there are many more who do not claim out of a false sense of dignity. Do you think that invading their dignity in that way, invading their privacy, is the best way to deal with a great human problem?" Well, I didn't think so ten days ago and I don't think so now.

To those who seek independence in outlook, justice and equality in industry and society – essential elements of trade unionism – the problem of an inbuilt subservient mentality tends to remain, a mentality demonstrated, in a sense, in the recent events in the GCHQ [Government Communiations Headquarters]. How else can you explain that free-born British people would sign away their rights to free trade unionism, to obey 'she who must be obeyed'? There's something wrong yet with our society: a mentality, in a sense, born out of centuries of slavery and serfdom.

Yet the massive changes in technology which have taken place do provide the basis for a tremendous leap forward in attitudes and ideas. The technological and scientific changes have been so considerable that potential changes will be even more revolutionary in terms of the destruction of jobs. A substantial proportion of our present-day four million unemployed is due to the new technology and the numbers will increase drastically. Consider, for example, the impact of the microchip which can be applied in just about every working situation, not just in factories, but in offices, in warehouses, in shops, everywhere where people work. They are being used in assembly because they enable machines to be taught quite complicated tasks. A lot of processes are being affected: measuring, weighing, filling and packaging, quality control, sorting, batching, welding and spraying. The robot-built car is not just a TV advertising gimmick, it's a fact of life. Many maintenance routines have become redundant and microelectronic checks can be made for all machinery so that faults can be quickly detected and even automatically corrected. Microelectronics are having an increasing effect on skilled work like machining. Machine tools can be instructed electronically to machine delicate parts using sensors and measuring equipment. Numerically controlled machine tools are being used extensively, and the microprocessor generation of these machines is coming in rapidly, enough to make old engineers weep and young people shiver with apprehension.

Huge numbers of jobs will go in the white-collar field, ranging from the drawing office to supervision. The idea that losses in employment in manufacturing and heavy industry will be offset by jobs in the service sector is no longer valid. Jobs in education, the social services, public administration, banks and insurance, all of them are under attack. The job of the typist is as vulnerable as that of the docker and the engineer. 40 per cent of office jobs will go as a result of the microchip because it threatens the typing pool, the accounting department, the wages department, and dozens of other occupations. In the shops, too, the chip is leading to great changes.

Talk of new industries providing masses of jobs, enough for the millions who are now unemployed, is a massive deception – it's an absolute fraud. Of course, some jobs will be there, but relatively few compared to the masses who will be unemployed. Repeatedly, we have been told how beneficial to mankind all these remarkable changes are or will be, but we should remember that the origin of microelectronics was not to provide work; it was to meet the demands of the military for space exploration and in the arms race. Benefits to working people were definitely not a consideration when these things were invented.

Technological change is the cause of great apprehension, great anxiety, tension amongst millions because of the threat to employment and not least to young people who've never had a job. Labour-saving devices were blamed for unemployment and poverty by workers here in what Noonan called Mugsborough (that was the name he gave Hastings) in a chapter entitled 'The Exterminating Machines'. Don't forget this was about 1906. Crass, the foreman, said:

> "These things can't be altered. You can't expect there can be plenty of work for everyone with all these 'ere labour-savin' machinery what's been invented....Machinery is the real cause of all the poverty."

The response of Frank Owen, the socialist, was very clear. He said,

> "Machinery is undoubtedly the cause of unemployment ...but it's not the cause of poverty: that's another matter altogether."
> [**p 105-6**, p 100]

Owen's remedy was the redistribution of wealth through socialism. The case for that remedy is very much stronger today that it was then, and that in essence is Robert Noonan's message for our time. All the great new technology should mean more wealth, not less. If wealth was reasonably distributed it would mean enough for everybody, and if employment was reasonably distributed it would mean jobs for everybody. There could be more leisure for most people than they now enjoy, a much less enforced leisure time for the people who are at present unemployed.

In his day, Noonan put the position with great force. He wrote:

> This is the position:
> It is admitted that never before in the history of mankind was it possible to produce the necessaries of life in such abundance as at present.
> The management of the affairs of the world...is at present in the hands of Practical, Level-headed, Sensible Business-men.
> The result of their management, is that the majority of the people find it a hard struggle to live...
> When the Practical, Level-headed, Sensible Business-men are asked why they do not remedy this state of things, they reply that they do not know what to do! or, that it is impossible to remedy it!
> And yet it is admitted that it is now possible to produce the necessaries of life, in greater abundance than ever before!
> [**pp 377-8** , pp 347-8]

Well, times haven't changed those essentials very much in eighty years. The practical, level-headed, sensible businessmen, and at least one woman, are running the country and they are running the Common Market. Our clever businessmen are more concerned with making money that with making things. That was the declared philosophy of the businessman, Jim Slater, some years ago. It seems to be the accepted view of the businessmen and the Government of today. Mrs Thatcher in 1984 could be echoing the words of A P Herbert in 1934 when he said, "Steel's gone to glory, cotton's gone in the shade, but we've still got the money-lending trade."

In what remains of British industry, there have been enormous changes. British workers *have* accepted automation, they *have* accepted mechanisation of mining and agriculture, they *have* accepted computers, they *have* accepted containers and they *have* accepted the microchip. But producing more with less has contributed in no small way to mass unemployment. The question is how long can we avoid a social explosion while unemployment continues at its present terrifying level? Division in society will become greater if we are faced, as a permanent feature, with an elite at work and masses without work. Even Prince Charles the other day began to recognise that unemployment amongst young people is the cause of much of the mugging and vandalism. Growing unemployment and cuts in the educational and social services are a blind and reactionary response to the challenge of economic and technological events. The scenario, as harsh as the bitter days of *The Ragged Trousered Philanthropists*, is before us now: profits before people, monetarism before common sense – that's what we are faced with.

There is only one answer: it's the socialist principle of 'one for all and all for one'. I remember when I was a lad being taken by my mother to the local Co-op quarterly meeting and over the platform used to be the slogan, 'each for all and all for each'. It's always remained with me because it seems to make sense. It means in essence, yes, a larger workforce, more people at work employed for shorter times, enjoying life more. A major task would be to ensure that the increased leisure means more happiness and that it could be the opening of a door to a better life for all.

Socialists (particularly in the WEA) believe that all people should be taught to enjoy education, hobbies and the arts, in all its forms, and of course travel. But we must have the wealth to enjoy these things, a view frequently expressed by Ernest Bevin in his day. He said, "Education creates aspirations and the love of the beautiful, but it is no use without having the means to enjoy it." By a more equal distribution of the wealth of the country, everyone would be able to enjoy leisure with the spread of knowledge, the light of understanding. A new civilisation could be constructed. It is no dream! True, the workers in Noonan's 'Cave' lacked confidence in their own class. They poured scorn on those who wanted to raise them out of their poverty: "they ridiculed and opposed and cursed and abused" those who wanted to build a better society [**p 424**, p 389]. But Noonan's characters, Owen and Barrington, held to their belief in socialism.

The socialist movement and the trade unions have grown beyond what Robert Noonan might have thought possible. Despite the shortcomings and the diseases of subservience and apathy, we are on the move. Noonan wrote of the workmen in Mugsborough: 'They often said that such things as leisure, culture, pleasure and the benefits of civilisation were never intended for the "likes of us". [**p 424**, p 389] Unfortunately, the knowledge of art and culture is still too much of a dead letter for millions of working people.

But the means to change are within our grasp. The working class that Noonan described had faith neither in themselves, in unions nor in their own destiny. True, Owen and Barrington, those splendid, upright characters in the book, pointed the way to socialism. What was missing was the message of uniting together, of fighting together. The workers needed to be organised and united and shaken out of their apathy. Shortly after the book was written, Ernie Bevin was leading unemployed demonstrations in Bristol. There had been a major dock strike in 1889. Bob Noonan died in Liverpool in February, 1911 and a few months afterwards a major strike swept the whole of Liverpool led by Tom Mann. If Bob Noonan had lived, doubtless his spirit would have been lifted and his confidence in his own class might well have been restored. The book's message would have been stronger.

Alongside the need to build a socialist movement, trade unionism – the organisation of working people at work – must be built. The person who advocates socialism, as Bob Noonan did, but fails to organise in trade unionism fails in the purpose. Equally, the working man or woman who is content merely to be a trade unionist and to organise on the industrial front is the same as a boxer fighting with one arm tied behind his back.

Thus, if we're going to achieve for ourselves today that freedom from unemployment and poverty which was the curse of Noonan's day and are evils with us today, if we are going to ensure a bright future for our children and their children, if we are going to ensure peace in the world, if we are going to be true to the traditions of the men and women of Tolpuddle (when 150 years ago six men of Dorset were transported to Australia for the simple act of wanting to organise in a trade union), we must build a stronger Labour Party combined with strong unions to do all these things so that we can fight with two hands. Today, the labour movement is under attack. It's been forced onto the defensive and must begin to take the counter-offensive. All-out efforts must be made to eliminate the apathy and the doubt, in the workplace and in the neighbourhood.

The simple, direct language of Robert Noonan provides a pattern to be adapted to modern needs for employed and unemployed people, to understand the vision of socialism, and then to organise, not only politically but industrially too. The alternative is a bleak future of mass unemployment and big business dictatorship presiding over a Taiwan-type of economy in our country.

In my view, we need to bring to life the hopes and the aspirations of Bob Noonan and all the pioneers of our movement. As Tom Mann would have said in his time: "Let no-one lose confidence, let's go forward – onward and upward to the better times ahead".

A Spiritual Elect?
Robert Tressell and the Early Socialists

Raphael Samuel

16 March 1985, Falaise Hall, Hastings.

In celebration of his 80th birthday, Fred Ball was presented with a miner's lamp by the labour movement in Hastings.

The lecture that I am going to give today is quite an uncomfortable one for people here who are socialists because it is about the apartness, or minority character, of socialists and how that is imprinted in Tressell's novel. There was a fine lecture in this series by Raymond Williams talking about the particular quality of Tressell's work as somebody who lived on the edge or at the margin of working-class life rather than within it. I want to pursue that line today, not so much by looking at Tressell's text in detail – I assume that people here will know it – but rather through some contexts.

I should say that I do believe that this is one of the great texts of our literature. It's to be compared with *Pilgrim's Progress*, and I find it moving that this book has survived through the minority enthusiasm of individual workers, of whom Fred Ball is an outstanding example.

Tressell's book is a miracle of survival. It was almost buried because it was published almost on the eve of the First World War and not under socialist auspices, and it could very well have been buried along with a great mass of social and socially-minded literature of that time. There are numbers of now forgotten novels, for example, by Allen Clarke the Lancashire novelist, quite a considerable novelist, which are unknown in literature or in working-class reading. There were great numbers of communist and socialist novels between the Wars; some of them are currently being reprinted by Lawrence and Wishart, for example, Harold Heslop.

But there are only two texts which have survived as major works of literature from worker-writers, one is *The Ragged Trousered Philanthropists* and the other is Lewis Grassic Gibbon's *A Scot's Quair*. Both those books have an increasing following, and I think it is interesting to speculate on why that should be so. One of the qualities in Tressell's, which differentiates it from almost all other socialist imaginative literature, is that it is a deeply pessimistic work. It has the hope of socialism at the end, but Tressell had a thorough-going realism about the obstacles that socialist advocacy had to face and, above all, the ways in which socialism came up against the working-class conservatism of the time. It is not a comforting book for socialism, as a result.

It is very much like a Pilgrim's Progress of our time, in which the lonely seeker after salvation finds himself beset by weakness and temptation on all sides. The language used by the building workers in the Cave is language that those of us who have occasion to advocate socialism or communism or Marxism today will recognise. All those arguments about human nature, all those arguments – about which Owen is so sarcastic – about how God ought not to have invented foreigners, are ones that we encountered alas only a year and a half ago at the time of the Falklands expedition. So it's this absolute truthfulness to the isolation of socialists which, I think, accounts in part for the great appeal which Tressell's book has in the labour and trade union movement today, because in some sense Owen's position in Mugsborough corresponds to the often lonely, isolated, embattled and, I think it has to be said, sometimes morally superior position in which individual socialists find themselves.

I want to begin by a few general remarks about socialists as seeing themselves as a people apart. Socialism, as an idea, is committed to equality and the democratisation of power and the self-determination of working people. And yet typically, socialists – at whatever time you choose to look at the history of the socialist movement, whether in the 1830s or in Tressell's period or I think today – have seen themselves as a minority elect. In one version – very much that of people like the Hastings members of the SDF [Social Democratic Federation] – they were salvationists bringing light into dark places, redemptionists carrying out rescue work among the masses. Or, like the early Fabians, they were a clerisy, representing the advanced and progressive thought of the day, the bearers of enlightenment. The more revolutionary socialists have typically constituted themselves as a vanguard. That's most familiar in the case of the Communist parties, but it is also true of the syndicalist movement of the 1910s and 1920s, and I think it's also true of many constituency activists in the Labour Party and the new kind of Labour councillor today, fanning the flames or sowing the seeds of discontent. The whole idea of Leninism, of Russian Communism, was of the Party, whether conceived of as an intelligentsia or as a cadre of professional revolutionaries, bringing understanding from outside to the people. I think there are real affinities between that idea of socialism and the very English idea of Sidney and Beatrice Webb and the Fabians in which it was the privilege of the professional classes, devoted to the public service and the public service ethic, who would plan and administer to the common good. The will to lead is one which has been very strong both in reformist and in revolutionary versions of socialism.

The sources of this apartness, of this vanguardism, are multiple, I think. They come in part from socialism's inheritance from the French Revolution, from Jacobinism and from those secret societies and revolutionary conspiracies and brotherhoods and clubs in which the socialist idea was born in France, and in Germany in the 1830s and '40s, or in groups like the Owenites in England. Marx and Engels drafted *The Communist Manifesto* for a small group of German tailors in exile, and one of the organisations which Marx formed or took part in 1850 was a head committee for the world revolution. It was also the leading idea of Blanqui, the great revolutionist. The whole idea of the professional revolutionary, the person who lived for the revolution, is something which descends from the French Revolution of 1789 and goes on through the Paris Commune and continues in the world Communist movement that issues from 1917. So, one source of vanguardism or socialists as a people apart comes from the Jacobin idea of revolutionary virtue, of the Incorruptibles like Robespierre in the French Revolution, and those who would withstand the temptations of worldliness and bring about a reign of virtue.

Another quite different source of socialist vanguardism, I think, is Christianity and the fact that socialism was born as a new Christianity (this is what Saint-Simon calls it), that socialism's working-class adherents in particular have often come from a deep religious culture, and that one of the ways in which socialists conceptualised themselves was as spiritual leaders and guides. Now, Tressell is different from perhaps other English socialists of his time – if I recall from Fred Ball's biography, in that his family origin may have been Catholic on his mother's side, rather than Protestant. In fact, it was a very deep Protestantism and above all Nonconformity which is the formative culture, the moral capital on which English socialism draws. So there are many affinities, indeed in my opinion, homologies, analogies, likenesses, between the socialist mission of the 1880s and 1890s and the Salvation Army. Frank Smith, who was General Booth's right-hand man in the Salvation Army, joins the socialist movement of the time and becomes Keir Hardie's closest friend. If you think of the salvationist orator going to the street corner with his or her words of blood and fire and think of the socialist orators of the same period, you are inhabiting a very similar mental universe. I think you cannot overestimate both the closeness of socialism's relation to Christianity and also the way in which socialists conceptualised themselves very much, as late Victorians did, as making war against an evil, contaminating world, like in the wonderful passage of Tawney's *Religion and the Rise of Capitalism* talking about seventeenth-century puritans as being soldiers in hostile territory surrounded with manifest terrors and evil, even the forces of the devil.

A third source of this apartness of socialists, or the idea of socialists as an elect or as a vanguard, comes from an idea in art which was born in the 1850s and '60s, the idea of art as representing the forces of beauty and truth against the vulgarity and degradation and corruption of a commercial society. It was an idea which had an eloquent advocate in John Ruskin who was one of the principal intellectual influences on the socialist movement in this country. In France, in Baudelaire, in the symbolist poets, and the Parnassians, there was an idea of the writer or poet as representing the values of art against the materialism and corruption of the bourgeoisie. Now, this was very important for Tressell and indeed for working-class socialists because the typical working man (and I'm afraid it was mostly working men rather than working women, though there were many women in the early socialist movement, but they weren't characteristically from the working class) who joined the socialist movement of the 1880s and 1890s is the 'artistic' kind of workman – of whom Tressell is the very type (as you know from his mural that was rescued).

One of our colleagues interviewed Fenner Brockway. He was talking about the Kentish Town branch of the SDF when he joined it. They weren't exactly intellectuals; they were more kind of "artistic". They were people who craved beauty in their lives. There is a wonderful description of a man called Anderson, the Finsbury Park Impossibilist who held forth at Finsbury Park night after night in the 1900s, and somebody who was recruited to socialism by him, Ralph Fox, says he listened to him month after month and suddenly he realised that this man didn't want to change anything. What he wanted to do was to produce beautiful words – word-pictures – of a wonderful future of absolute harmony. It was a kind of compensation for the misery of his work by day in a motorcycle factory, and that was sufficient unto itself. An awful lot of socialist energy in the 1890s and 1900s was spent preaching and offering beautiful word-pictures of the socialist future or even more beautiful pictures of the medieval or primitive communist past, as Tressell does through Owen in *The Ragged Trousered Philanthropists* when he talks about the fifteenth century, the golden age of the artisan.

A lot of socialism could be seen as a kind of displaced artistic activity. I think there is some example of that in the current miners' strike, with the enormous upsurge of creativity normally thwarted in the pit villages and the huge outpouring of poetry which is one of the ways in which the miners, if you go to pit villages, have expressed what their strike is about. Socialism provided one kind of outlet for all that normally buried artistic impulse within the working class. But together with that, I think, went a profound sense – which you get in *The Ragged Trousered Philanthropists* – that if art is beautiful, surrounding life is ugly. And working-class life is sordid, and so a sense of carrying the values of art is something that sets you off against those surroundings rather than making you sympathetic to them. The idea of destroying, the idea of being in a living hell – I mean hell because of its denial of art as much as because of its poverty – I think, is one of the driving forces of working-class people who become socialist in that time.

This character of socialists as a people apart is also something that you come upon in the Labour Party between the wars. Amazingly, the kind of people who became Labour councillors in the 1920s and 1930s thought of themselves as being stewards for people who were too weak to help themselves. So the Labour Party built itself as a kind of paternalism in the localities. There are some very interesting films that were discovered recently by the Bermondsey, South East London Labour Party in the 1920s; they were campaigning pictures for public health. Among other things, they showed the hop pickers in their huts, in their insanitary conditions and in their enjoyment of the September holiday, and then you saw the Labour councillors coming down to help them in their wage demands and to make their conditions a bit more sanitary. And they are a different race; they're in suits and ties, they are well intentioned and benevolent, but definitely of a different species-being.

Again, if you think of the women of the Co-operative Women's Guild, part of the force of the Labour Party between the wars in working-class areas was that of the woman who joined the Guild (which was a mass organisation at the time) who was a kind of missionary of enlightenment. She was the person who had the knowledge – above all, the knowledge – of birth control and the new labour-saving devices which could rescue working-class women from endless child-rearing and from the drudgery of the kitchen. She represented in herself a principle of hope. I remember talking to somebody who joined the Labour theatre group in Hackney in East London and what she remembered was that Kath Duncan, an elementary school teacher who was there, had mauve curtains – sixty years later there was still a note of wonder in her voice that someone could have something so daring as mauve curtains, in contrast to the drabness of working-class or lower-middle-class respectability. Kath represented, as it were, modern living. Marion Philips, the National Women's Secretary of the Labour Party, wrote a book in 1921 on the labour-saving home. Labour people believed they had the knowledge that could rescue people from the drudgery of the nineteenth century. So again it's a sense of being outsiders, helping people, bringing light into dark places. Within a poor street would be the Labour family that could manage, who had ambitions for their children to have some education; they were people of the community but also in some way apart from it, different. And one could go into the ways in which socialists today, even more strikingly, whether in the trade union movement or in the Labour Party, are in some way different from the people whom they can see themselves as serving.

I want to talk about the particular historical period of English socialism in which Tressell joins the Hastings Branch of the SDF and *The Ragged Trousered Philanthropists* is written. There was enormous social distance between socialists and the people that they were serving and in whose interests they were agitating. It's spectacular in the case of a gentleman turned agitator, like Henry Hyndman, the leader of the SDF, and in those patricians who joined the Fabian Society in the 1880s or people like Bernard Shaw and Sidney and Beatrice Webb. Just to give you an example of this social distance: in 1886 there was a spontaneous camp-out of the unemployed in Trafalgar Square, thousands of unemployed in a bad winter congregating there. The Socialist League, which was the most revolutionary socialist organisation of that time, founded by William Morris, Eleanor and Edward Marx-Aveling and patronised by Frederick Engels, for a month they couldn't decide whether they should actually send a speaker down to the unemployed because this was a class below the level at which respectable, even revolutionary, politics was possible – this was called the 'lumpenproletariat'. The social distance between the artisan on the one hand and the poor on the other was so immense that even leading socialists whose mission it was to agitate amongst them drew back. It was in fact a matter of pride amongst socialists of all stripes, revolutionists or reformists, right up to 1920, that the person who supported the socialists or who voted for the Independent Labour Party was the artisan, not the slum poor. The slum poor, like the half-drunks in Tressell's book, are the people who are Tories. The working man who votes Tory doesn't think. It was the the thinking working man who supported the Labour cause. Right up to and including the elections in which the slums actually began to return Labour councillors, for example, in the Gorbals in Glasgow, the local Labour party wouldn't actually recognise it was having support from the lower depths. Labour's ideal constituency was the thinking working class, the artisan.

So there was a tremendous sense of distance between socialists and the poor. This was true not only of the early socialist political movement but also of the New Unionism, the organisation of unskilled workers. The matchgirls' strike, one of the historic events in English trade unionism, was organised by Annie Besant, a woman who had the courage to desert her clergyman husband and lived independently, and Herbert Burroughs, who was a civil servant. Then, think of the London Dock Strike of 1889. That was led by two quintessential Victorian artisans: Tom Mann, whose political apprenticeship was served as a Shakespearean (he formed the Shakespearean Mutual Improvement Society of Chiswick), who had travelled to Paris, a man of great respectability, a vegetarian – very different from an East London docker; and John Burns, who would take his wife on a Saturday night to the opera, a very cultivated engineer and artisan. Or think of the gasworkers, who were indeed led by a gasworker, Will Thorne, but whose advisor was Eleanor Marx-Aveling, Karl Marx's daughter, or the famous Manningham Mills strike in Bradford in 1890 or thereabouts where it was Isabella Ford, an elementary school teacher, and Tom Maguire, a photographer's assistant (and, like Tressell, another consumptive working-class writer) who were the original leaders. So trade unionism at this time, in so far as it was beginning to become a mass trade unionism, also comes from people who weren't the same as those whom they were leading.

Not only was there a social difference between socialists and the people whom they led and appealled to, but the very fact of their socialist activity made them socially further apart. Annie Besant was a pariah to respectable society because she had abandoned her husband, but to the workgirls of Bryant & May in Bow Common, East London, she was a great lady. And one of the things that her participation in the socialist movement did was to actually elevate her status, not with that intention, but because that was the effect of the enormous social gulfs of that time. There was a whole process of cultural upgrading which participation in the socialist movement involved, above all for working-class recruits. It was the historic character of socialist and later on of communist movements that they were workers' universities. People might join the socialist movement for the most instrumental of reasons, because of a strike or because of poverty or whatever, but the fact is that political activity is an intensely intellectual activity. It involved continuous argument; it involved inevitably and immediately arguments of a kind wonderfully rehearsed in *The Ragged Trousered Philanthropists* about human nature; it involved, for those who are free thinkers, giving testimony against God; it involved knowing the Bible better than those whom you had to combat.

The socialist inevitably became a bookish kind of person, so socialism partly appeals to the bookworms amongst the working class. But even if you are not a bookworm, you become one by nature of the political activity itself and all that intellectual practice which was the very stuff of socialism which was mainly advocacy. So to become a debater, to become a speaker, was required of you, even if you didn't get up on the platform. That would be so in the workplace. So inevitably the socialist working man becomes, as Owen in *The Ragged Trousered Philanthropists* was referred to sarcastically, the "Professor". A little while ago, a very far left organisation indeed, the Revolutionary Workers' Party, a Trotskyist organisation, expelled one of their members, a shop steward in Oxford, from their ranks, and they wrote a pamphlet to denounce him and the main error that he was condemned for was neo-Kantianism. In other words, he was perpetrating a German philosophical heresy of the 1900s. So this whole way in which many people complain about socialists, that they speak a language which other people can't understand, comes from this kind of intellectuality which is a part of the ordinary practice of the socialist movement. What it means is both that the socialist movement of that time reproduced the existing social divisions of society, that is, it was recruited mainly from the kind of working person who could cope, who had some education, but also that it then set up divisions of its own. The very fact of becoming a socialist set socialists apart from their fellow workers.

Now, I think Tressell unconsciously and unintendedly structures his own book around that. Owen is the one working man in *The Ragged Trousered Philanthropists* who speaks standard English. Owen doesn't speak a dialect, a Sussex version of cockney. He speaks the English of any literature of the day. The other workers speak in wonderfully memorable language, a language so idiomatic and so close to the heart of popular feeling that you could reproduce much of the dialogue without embarrassment today for its contemporary form. The only words that are outdated are Owen's, and, though you may agree as I do with the sentiment, the actual way in which they are phrased is very literary. So in other words, what I am suggesting is that implicitly Tressell is recognising the gulf linguistically between the socialists and other people. Owen is a propagandist. But there were socialists of the time who seem to be concerned less with persuading others than in showing the banner, people who nursed their socialism as a private passion, who weren't actually concerned to spread the word or to convert as much as to display their own moral or intellectual superiority.

Another way in which what I have been talking about can be seen in *The Ragged Trousered Philanthropists* is the very deep sense of artistic outrage that Tressell as a craftsman felt about that slosh work. Some of the finest passages in the book are about scamping, the interest only in profit, the fact that pumice stone, he said, is something that painters will no longer use because you no longer rub down the surfaces – you are just told to "slosh", he says, to "slosh the stuff on". Remember the many passages where, when he has a chance to exercise his own suppressed artistic talent, for Rushton and the others this is simply a means to make a profit, and Owen's indignation as a craftsman, which I think is exactly Tressell's own, at what the building trade was and what it ought to be whenever there was a chance to employ Moorish decorative work. He had a lovely conceit about this; he erected an imaginary memorial of pumice stone, formerly used by housepainters. He was himself, you remember, apprenticed to one of the old-style builders who had a sense of craftsmanship, before sweating and the like.

So I think you can see, what I was trying to refer to before, the particular appeal of socialism to the sense of artistic outrage at the ugliness of capitalism, which is common to both working-class socialists of that time and also to middle- and upper-class socialists. It's the very basis of William Morris' socialism – capitalism is ugly. I think one of the difficulties we have now in relating to socialists of that time is their wholesale condemnation of the urban environment. Morris, embarrassingly for those of us who are campaigning to defend the Greater London Council, wanted to destroy London physically. He wanted there to be a great annual festival to observe the destruction of East London and its replacement by forests – something which seems to be more a vision of the Conservative Party today than of those on the left. Morris takes it for granted that city life and all the artefacts of capitalism are ugly. So does Owen in *The Ragged Trousered Philanthropists*. This sense that everything commercial is ugly, that there are artistic values which are minority ones that are being overwhelmed by commerce was, I think, a very important part of the socialist imagination until very recently.

The socialist mission of the 1880s and 1890s had very close affinities to what was called at the time rescue work. We know it best through the Salvation Army and through General Booth's *In Darkest England*. General Booth has a most dramatic picture at the front of his book showing the drunks, the out-of-works, people being pulled down into a slough of despond, and then the helping hand of the rescue of the Salvation Army and its labour colonies. I think that idea of the life of the poor as a pit of both oppression and of infamy is one which socialists share. And indeed the socialist idea was born at the same time as the modern word 'slum' was born. The idea of slumming was born in 1883, at the same time as Oxford and Belgravia were swept by a craze for slumming, people going down into the lower depths in places like East London.

Socialism also has affinities to the imperialist idea of the white man's burden. Imperialism itself at the time wore a moral garb. The empire-builders weren't going out to India or to Suez or Africa or Sudan or South Africa for profit. They were going out in the way that missionaries believed themselves to be going out, in order to help those who were incapable of helping themselves. I think that socialists in their own way, working-class as much as middle-class or upper-class, conceived themselves as bearing a burden of the world. The kind of working man who becomes a socialist in this period, like Tressell or like Fred Jowett of Bradford, would not be the person who would be himself in the lowest depths but a person who would be aware that there were people around the corner who had children who had no shoes on their feet, a family at the end of the street who couldn't cope because the husband was always drinking. So it was very much a kind of rescue work, going as it were from the strong to help the weak, very much in the way in which the Salvation Army went out. And again, Owen; it isn't that he is materially better off than his fellows, but culturally he is an aristocrat, isn't he, in *The Ragged Trousered Philanthropists*, an aristocrat who's giving his life to helping to enlighten them in their darkness.

A great deal of early socialist activity was, in fact though not in name, philanthropic. One of the main activities of the Clarion League – which was the mass organisation of young men and women who went cycling every weekend, when they weren't romantically preaching the word of socialism on the village green which is what they did on Sundays, or subversively brandishing their knapsacks and their flasks in front of the respectable churchgoers on church parade – was what were called Cinderella Clubs. Cinderella Clubs used to hold Christmas and other parties for the slum children, very much like the kind of effort that local Labour parties gave for miners' children this last Christmas. That was the main activity of the Clarion League Cinderella Clubs. And the Marxist Social Democratic Federation, when it wasn't preaching the inevitability and necessity of revolution, was setting up soup kitchens in poor districts and agitating for work for the unemployed. There was a lot of charitable work, though not in name, that entered into the practice in the socialist mission.

Socialism got rooted in this country because socialists took up the cause of the most helpless. The socialists who were elected to the Board of Guardians campaigned for the orphan children not to have the stigma of wearing the workhouse uniform, for them to have cottage homes, for them to have toys. Or like Graham Wallas, who was on a School Board, socialists campaigned for there to be flowers in the elementary schools to bring some beauty into the lives of the poor. The earliest campaign was on school milk and school feeding – a great plank of socialist agitation in the 1900s – bitterly opposed on the grounds that if the schools provided the children with meals, it would undermine parental responsibility, very similar arguments to the ones used by critics of welfare today. There were all kinds of very practical ways in which socialists presented themselves as bringing help and protection to the needy, to those unable to help themselves.

Socialists saw themselves, whatever their social position – working-class, bourgeois, aristocratic – during these years, as spokesmen for the most helpless poor. They had a chivalresque idea of themselves, and indeed the language of chivalry, of knight errantry, of crusading, is one that you find in socialist oratory of the period. Shaw's Major Barbara is a Salvationist, but really she could equally have been a socialist of that period, for the way in which she sees her mission. Industrially, also, the socialists and trade unionists of the period are concerned above all with the more helpless industrial worker, with the sweated trades, with the dangerous trades, the trades where people would die after a few years because of poisoning, as in the white lead trade in East London or phosphorus work and the match trade, the sweated shopworker, the laundrywoman, the un-unionised, the casual labourer and above all the unemployed. It was a matter of the strong helping the weak – a trade union principle, as well as an aristocratic one of *noblesse oblige*.

The socialist support for the suffragettes and the women's movement – the suffragette movement, it's worth recalling, was formed within the Independent Labour Party – also had some of that character of chivalry. For Keir Hardie, who was an ardent supporter of women's suffrage, or George Lansbury, women were seen as the weaker, as the victim of society, being helped by those men who took up the women's cause.

I think the socialist movement of the 1880s also had very strong affinities with the social purity movements of the time, with the crusades against moral corruption, of the kind that Josephine Butler had pioneered in the campaign on the Contagious Diseases Act in the 1870s. There was a very strong temperance component in early socialism and indeed in early communism. There was a temperance group of Labour MPs right down to the end of the 1920s. There were dry housing estates, Labour housing estates, continuing right to the end of the 1950s, and bitter divisions within Labour parties between the temperance advocates and others. But in many ways socialism was conceived of as a kind of moral cleansing of society. Capitalism was a corrupt and contaminating society, and I'd remind you that some of the powerful passages in *The Ragged Trousered Philanthropists* are the accounts of the besotted, of the drunken, the Cricketers' Arms as one absolute pit of human weakness and depravity. It's because his writing transcends as well as represents his politics that he can actually convey those music-hall songs that he does wonderfully, in ways that you can actually (if you feel sympathetic to music-hall, as probably most of us would nowadays) still respond to. But recall that he is giving this as an example of human stupidity, that these are absurd ditties on which people are regaling themselves and stopping themselves seeing the truth. So, *The Ragged Trousered Philanthropists* isn't written as a book of a temperance advocate, and we have the character of Slyme to show his own sense of how partial and hypocritical the merely Christian or the merely temperant would be. But the fact is that, in his own way, it is a very powerful advocacy against drink, and in that I think he's of the socialism of his time.

I want to end up by saying something about mysticism, because I think this also has a bearing on Tressell and on the socialism of that time. It is arguable that socialism in all its different versions, among other things, represents a kind of displaced religious longing. It is a common accusation against socialism (or communism) that it is a kind of religion. I don't want to enter into that now, but to say about the particular period that I am talking about that whatever their particular crotchets, whether they were evolutionists or revolutionists, Fabians or SDFers or ILPers, those who came to socialism in these years embraced it with the rapture of a new-found faith. Socialism was not only historically inevitable, it was also, in Annie Besant's expressive phrase, "ethically beautiful". It offered not only a more equitable mode of economic organisation, but also a philosophy of life: "a noble practical religion, a true solidarity of interests, a morality of the higher self". It called on men and women to transcend the immediate necessities of existence and take on larger views. Quite interestingly, in socialist feminism of the period and in socialist support for feminism and the emancipation of women, there was an ideal of transcending sexuality, that sexuality degraded, an idea which you get very often in the socialist marriages of the period, a true spiritual, platonic companionship, very often of childless marriages, like those of Sidney and Beatrice Webb and other Fabians; the idea that the only way of rescuing a woman from her degradation was to rescue her from her sex – that was also a very strong idea that many suffragettes had – and that it was by rising to a higher plane of spiritual being that people could find real freedom and real companionship.

And a part of that was also – and this was a working-class idea as well as an upper- or middle-class idea – the appeal of the simple life, that what was wrong with society was that there was too much luxury, too many goods, too much busy-ness and that the route to social salvation was by a radical simplification of life. The first class in sociology at Ruskin College in 1899 was of the kind that must have been captivating to impecunious, young working-class bachelors trying to persuade potential mothers and fathers-in-law that they were a good match. It divided human needs into two kinds; the first kind is companionship, warmth, love, art – that was primary; things like crockery, tablecloths, household furniture were contingent and secondary. In other words, it was the things of the spirit that mattered. That was the kind of ideal that was being put before young working-class students at Ruskin at that time.

There was also a middle- and upper-class version of that, of those who, like Charlotte Wilson, abandoned life in stockbroker Hampstead and went to live in the simplicity of a farm on the edge of Hampstead Heath, or those who built the first garden city at Letchworth. A lot of the Fabian mission to the middle class in the 1890s was to tell them that they didn't need so many domestic servants – you could get by with one domestic servant or, if you were really revolutionary like Edward Carpenter, none at all. This is one of the ways in which socialists were pioneers of modern living because if you simplified life, you didn't need domestic servants, you didn't need that kind of inequality. With this went a very strong religion of nature, which came partly from Walt Whitman, from American transcendentalism. It can be seen in the huge socialist enthusiasm for rambling and cycling which went on until quite recent times.

Although socialists of the period were very often in revolt against orthodox Christianity, one way of describing them is that they were spiritual vagrants. Quite often conversion to the socialist movement involved a kind of born-again religious practice. The socialism of the 1890s and 1900s was mixed up with various form of secularist religion and materialist mysticism. Tom Mann was a Swedenborgean; Kier Hardie, whom people remember for his deep-set, sunken, visionary look, was a practising spiritualist who communed with the spirits of the departed, as did his friend, Frank Smith; Herbert Burroughs, the Marxist co-organiser of the matchgirl strike, was a Theosophist; and the Fabians were honeycombed with Theosophists. Beyond those who were actually members of cults, there was also a kind of diffused (what is called) ethical socialism. Labour churches of the time constructed a kind of socialist alternative to, but also reproduction of, ceremonial religious practice and set up socialist Sunday schools as a kind of nursery of socialism.

Apart from such explicitly proto-religious and semi-religious practices, there were also some very deep mystical impulses in the socialism of that time. There was the idea, for example, that in becoming a socialist you transcended yourself, you ceased to be a person of the middle class or for that matter of the working class and you became transfigured and made anew. Stephen Yeo has written a very fine article in the *History Workshop Journal* called 'Socialism and the New Life: the Religion of Socialism in the 1880s and 1890s'. In autobiography after autobiography, you can read about the sense of personal salvation that becoming a socialist entailed. But apart from that, there were also the ways which socialists conceived history, the idea of there being invisible powers, invisible forces at work making for a socialist future – for Marxists, the succession of modes of production; for Fabians, the inevitability of collectivism. But the whole idea (which is a wonderful idea) that history is on your side was the basis of the socialist idea until about fifteen or twenty years ago. It gave tremendous confidence, even in the worst of conditions. History pointed in one way only – forwards. The idea that you were being carried as if you were on history's back and that you were realising a historical mission seems to me to be in essence a mystical idea.

In the ideas that socialists had of what the socialist state would be, you have also I think something which is very close indeed to a Christian idea of paradise. If you read William Morris' *News from Nowhere*, his socialist utopia set in the Thames Valley, it is a vision (it is one of the difficulties for us because our own imagination doesn't work like that in the late twentieth century) of absolute peace. The railways, which Morris hated almost as much as Mrs. Thatcher, disappeared and people travel on donkeys. The figures are of a dream; there are young maidens and patriarchal figures with grey beards. Everybody is at rest; there is complete amity and happiness. It's a picture of heaven and, like Milton's heaven, it's rather dull. But it is one where all contradiction has been resolved. Now, I think one of the real difficulties that we have is understanding (for those people who are socialists) how it was that an idea of absolute peace could be as appealing as that. What I think is beyond question is that, in the first place, it is a mystic vision. It isn't a development of things as they were. It was the world turned upside down; as there was energy, bustle, in the salesmen's term of the period, 'push' and commercialism, so under socialism you have the end of that.

I would like to end by quoting from the last paragraphs in *The Ragged Trousered Philanthropists*:

> The gloomy shadows enshrouding the streets, concealing for the time their grey and mournful air of poverty and hidden suffering, and the black masses of cloud gathering so menacingly in the tempestuous sky, seemed typical of the Nemesis which was overtaking the Capitalist System. That atrocious system which, having attained to the fullest measure of detestable injustice and cruelty, was now fast crumbling into ruin.....

And then there is Owen's vision of the co-operative commonwealth, this being striking because it's in such contrast, I think, to the social realism of the novel heretofore:

> But from these ruins was surely growing the glorious fabric of the Co-operative Commonwealth. Mankind, awakening from the long night of bondage and mourning and arising from the dust wherein they had lain prone so long, were at last looking upward to the light that was riving asunder and dissolving the dark clouds which had so long concealed from them the face of heaven. The light that will shine upon the world wide Fatherland and illumine

> the gilded domes and glittering pinnacles of the beautiful cities of the future, where men shall dwell together in true brotherhood and goodwill and joy. The Golden Light that will be diffused throughout all the happy world from the rays of the risen sun of Socialism.

That's the vision splendid of a Marxist, revolutionary socialist of the 1900s. And it is a mystical vision.

Tressell the Teacher

Tony Benn

31 May 1986, Falaise Hall, Hastings

It's a very great honour for me to be invited to give this lecture – and also to find what a very friendly, family atmosphere there is.

I feel in a way why I have to explain why I always have a new copy of Tressell. It's because I give away all my others and I haven't got a dog-eared copy left. Funnily enough, two days ago I was on a bus in London and there was nobody on top of the bus but myself and a couple of housepainters who had come straight off the job. I thought I would try and I asked the older one, "Have you ever heard of *The Ragged Trousered Philanthropists*?" "Ah," he said, "of course I have." He had a young lad with him, about nineteen, and he hadn't heard of it, and I knew that another copy of the book would go out.

I would like to turn to the question, Where does the book derive its power, how is that power exercised? because Robert Tressell never held elected office. He wasn't famous in his own lifetime and his reputation rests on one book, *The Ragged Trousered Philanthropists*, published after his death. In that book he chronicled in meticulous detail the daily experiences of working-class people and analysed the factors which explained what was happening to them, and this is what made him a socialist propagandist. For he sought to explain these factors to his contemporaries and to show them the role they might play in changing their own future. It is a book of great literary merit, revealing enormous powers of description, using a very vivid imagery, in marvellous style and with deep compassion. It is also a book of great historical importance because it describes conditions in Hastings at that time in the building trade and it touches on so many aspects of contemporary life that it would be a classic on those grounds alone.

But it is as a socialist classic that I want to speak of it this afternoon. It draws out of the experience which Tressell or Noonan himself had an understanding of the structure of the economy and of society which is immensely intelligible, though he had a lot of difficulty in persuading his contemporaries of its relevance. It is a book illuminated by hope and in that sense it is, and remains, an educational book, making its author into a great teacher. And it is of Tressell the teacher that I want to speak.

What are the barriers to an understanding of socialism that we normally come up against when we talk about it to those who are not socialists? For many people, it is too intellectual. They think of the great socialist classics which they haven't read, of the need to have a university degree perhaps to understand Karl Marx's *Das Kapital* or any of the other great writings. Socialism appears too sectarian because there's always a great argument going on, as with any faith that is growing, between one school of thought and another, and people are put off by it. Socialism is identified with bureaucracy because people think of local councils that have been socialist and of all the managerial aspects of it. Socialism appears to be too professionalised and too linked to careerism. Then there are nations which call themselves socialist which have fallen far short of the standards that Tressell would certainly have regarded as being essential. And socialism has been often too vilified to find it very easy to get an audience anyway.

Tressell's socialism suffers from none of these defects. It is direct, relating directly to what is happening to people that morning at work. It has a crystal clarity about it because nobody can be in any doubt as to what he is saying or why. It is illuminated by a very deep humanity because his feeling for the characters in his book can't possibly be forgotten. And it has a simplicity about it which helps to explain its appeal. This book has acquired a new urgency because the clock is now being turned back to Victorian times when the working class had to pay the price for the capitalist crisis. A few years ago this book might have been seen as a novel about the bad old days. Today it has a freshly contemporaneous ring.

Why, more than seventy years after the book was written, has so little advance been achieved by working people in Britain in their relationship to the structure of power in society, despite the existence of the biggest and strongest democratic socialist labour movement in the world which is officially committed to socialism and to the transformation of society? Was it that Tressell's ideas were tried and failed? Was it that they were not tried? Or were there other factors to it? I think it important to put these questions because some people have turned their back on socialism because they believe that all the things Tressell spoke of were tested and proved to be wrong, and so socialism has to be consigned to the scrap heap, while we move to the absolutely ultra-modern idea of monetarism, first invented by Adam Smith 200 years ago.

All the central economic issues that occupy our attention in 1986 were identified in some form or another by Tressell and weaved into his story. He dealt at great length with unemployment and its impact on those who experienced it or were threatened by it. He dealt with the profit motive and where it leads society if making money is all that matters and power attaches to those who make it. He points out the impact of low wages, now re-appearing in the Hong Kong-type economy which the present Government appear to wish to reintroduce.

Tressell is very explicit on the class struggle; analysis of the conflict of interest between those who own the wealth and those who actually create it could hardly be put more vividly. He also deals with the conflict between public and private ownership; the way the private owners of the Electricity Company managed to get a gas tax put on and drove the Gas Company outside the Borough limits and, as it did not make a profit, then municipalised so that the owners would not lose money from their investment – you could hardly have a more vivid example than that.

Tressell describes how the charitable trusts very quickly found the exercise of their function gave them a control over people which they found very pleasing. Today, the Welfare State has also become an instrument of social control. The book has also got some vivid accounts of local government and the way in which the City Fathers, helped by the estate agents on the planning committee, ran the community to meet their own needs. The problems of education, of school meals and housing are vividly described. And we read of the exploitation of women and youth, even the role of machinery, to explain why people were out of work and the extent to which tariff reform or free trade was better.

The role of the Churches, set against the ideas of revolutionary Christianity to which Tressell himself was attached, is identified, and the way in which some Anglican ministers have got around the challenge of the Sermon on the Mount by saying that, 'If only the rich were kind and the poor were patient, it would be all right when we we're dead.' The difference between that view and the view of John Ball and Tressell and indeed Jesus himself was that people said 'Why should we wait until we are dead?' The nature of the media is touched on through the *Obscurer* and the *Weekly Chloroform* – brilliantly titled – and how relevant that is! We learn about electoral politics under which people pursue office and then fraternise with their political opponents, so you get the sense that everyone at the top is working against everyone at the bottom. We learn about the relevance of civil liberties and the link between repression in Ireland and repression in Britain (as it is today), and about the use of troops and police to repress a strike in Yorkshire involving 400,000 miners, some of whom were killed by soldiers.

Tressell also refers to one socialist renegade and the way in which he justified his betrayal of socialism by moving socialism rather skilfully from the present into the future – what I would call a Clause Four approach to socialism: 'We're all for it, but later'. Indeed, the modern view of electoral politics is that if only the party is loyal and socialists would shut up it will be all right when there is a Labour government.

Every one of those issues is back on the agenda and if Tressell were alive today I find it hard to believe that he could understand how so little had changed. Nor, I think, would he be very impressed by the excuses offered as to why so little has changed. We are always hearing that circumstances do not allow socialist remedies to be applied. In Bristol, during the last General Election, a very, very old lady said to me, "When are we going to have socialism, Mr Benn, because when I was a child, we were told we could not have socialism because of the First World War; then it was the Balance of Payments; and now it is the Public Sector Borrowing Requirement? When are we going to have socialism?" And it was a very good question because, as she went through the reasons that had been given, you realised that they were all excuses for people who did not want to make a change rather than reasons why it had not been made.

Socialism is presented as extremist and we are told the working class has disappeared. But if there once was a sort of classical, historical, industrial working class that would give us socialism, why didn't it give us socialism when we had it? This argument is an excuse for saying it cannot be done.

There is another argument as to why we have not had socialism that I think Tressell would not have accepted either, which is the 'Scapegoat' theory: that it's because of certain individuals, like the present Prime Minister. I personally do not believe there is such a thing as 'Thatcherism'. The danger of this argument is it diverts you away from the socialist argument because if Mrs Thatcher were to retire or be booted out and was replaced by Tebbit and Tebbittism would that really actually make any difference? The danger of the scapegoat theory is that it diverts people from what it is really about. There is another version of that argument too – the 'Traitor' theory – that we never got socialism because Ramsay MacDonald or George Brown or Roy Jenkins let us down at the critical moment. Once you go for this theory you miss the point because if socialism is so fragile that it depends on the endorsement of famous men and women then we really are very weak.

Tressell did not have much time for the personality orientation of electoral politics, preferring to stick to the basic issues, analysis and the key role of the working class itself in bringing it about. Tressell always expressed his confidence in the capacity of the working class to liberate itself, despite all the setbacks and all the disappointments he experienced, all of which he sets out so clearly in his book. Therein lies the essential nature of his socialism and the optimism which sustained his vision.

Tressell's socialism was based on certain very clear commitments: to social morality,deeply influenced by the ethical message of Jesus, and to solidarity, to the recognition that workers had a common interest. Then there was his belief in democracy, in equality, in internationalism, and – this is what makes him such a teacher – his belief in the power of knowledge to change society by building self-confidence.

Why then didn't we have socialism? Because Labourism, operating a narrow electoralism within the unchanged structure of the bourgeois state under capitalism, and the Labour Party, which wasn't explicitly socialist, worked an very different principles than the ones that Tressell set out. It was, in part, paternalism – 'If only you had confidence in us, it would all be all right' – a Fabian idea that, as long as you could get power and manage it, it will be done. All this was combined with a fervent belief in 'ad hockery' – Harold Wilson's greatest term of abuse was what he would call a 'theological' argument, as if somehow analysis had little to offer in terms of the practice of a Labour Government. Labour often compromised and fudged and has been weak and intolerant. Nationalism has been an obstacle, as if the problems of Britain can be solved in isolation. And I think Labour has suffered from elitism and defeatism.

Now let me be quite clear, because I am giving a lecture, not making a political speech, that this criticism is an attempt at a clinical diagnosis of a long-term trend and not an attack on those, either now or over the years, who have held leadership positions in the labour movement. We are all, in some way, responsible for what went wrong, and we do have to go back over our own history, whether we like it or not, to understand why it is that so many gains made by the labour movement have proved to be so fragile and have been so easily taken away.

What went wrong? Let us take some of the factors which would require examination. Britain was the first industrialised nation in the world, and out of Britain come three of the most powerful economic philosophies which are now competing for world support: Adam Smith, in his *Wealth of Nations*, wrote about capitalism; Robert Owen, the first man ever to be called a socialist, was a benevolent industrialist and developed the idea of a Co-operative Commonwealth: and Marx, the communist, wrote about British capitalism. Britain developed a market-oriented economy in the British Empire where we sent out our troops to see that the colonies sold us cheap raw materials and bought the things we made. That was what imperialism was about, and the people who controlled those economic forces became very rich. But capitalism in Britain failed to develop technology and, because of the social structure, failed to develop the education necessary to make use of it. Britain fell behind Germany and the United States well over a hundred years ago because British capitalism was still encumbered by a feudal background. Capitalism was saved by rearmament between the wars, for public expenditure on weapons brought back full employment.

After the war, Britain experienced a boom because Germany, Italy and Japan had been defeated and that boom financed the Welfare State and strengthened labour because, under full employment, trade unions could bargain strongly with their employers. Thus was created what came to be known as Welfare Capitalism. Harold Macmillan had thought it all up in 1938 when he was a Tory backbencher in a book called *The Middle Way* which was well to the left of the Labour Party today. But the underlying decline went on and Britain's failure to invest continued and the internationalisation of capital, combined with the Common Market, the International Monetary Fund and so on, created circumstances where capitalism could no longer afford welfarism. This aspect is hardly ever discussed by the Labour Party.

One reason why Tressell's dream has never been realised is that the Labour movement has given up analysis to explain what is actually happening. And people don't know what is happening any more than they did when Tressell tried to explain it in this town before the First World War. Until we use the socialist tools of analysis, I don't think we are going to make much progress

A second problem arises from institutional obstacles, because, despite all that we are told, British institutions are very undemocratic. We have the three parts of the Constitution, the Crown, the Lords and the Commons. Now the Crown has only two residual personal powers. One is the right to dissolve Parliament, which at a critical moment could be used to disadvantage a Labour Government, as happened to Gough Williams in Australia. The other is the power to decide whom to call to form a Government, which could be very critical in the event of a hung Parliament. All the rest of the powers of the Crown have now been transferred to the Prime Minister, who therefore has powers of patronage on a monumental scale, for none of which are Prime Ministers responsible to Parliament. Then we have the Lords who are a wholly unelected body. The House of Commons has very little power over what is happening. I give as one classic example: Attlee never bothered to tell Parliament or for that matter the Cabinet that he was building the atom bomb. Mrs Thatcher didn't have to get the consent of the House of Commons before the Falklands War was launched.

We still have a medieval Parliament with enormous patronage within the hands of the Prime Minister who appoints Ministers or sacks them without consulting anyone, and appoints peers (seven Prime Ministers have put 600 people in Parliament), appoints all the bishops, appoints all the judges, appoints all the chairmen of the nationalised industries and appoints the chairman of the BBC. And we still go on uttering the magical phrase, that we are the 'Mother of Parliaments'. We are the most inadequate mother there ever was because actually we don't have control of the effective power. Behind this facade lies the Civil Service and military power boosted immensely by the huge arms budget. The real purpose of this is to strengthen the military vis-a-vis the working class in Britain. Most wars historically have been internal, as Field Marshal Lord Carver said when he retired.

Labour when in office has never done anything to change those institutional structures, preferring a consensus around the unchanged structures of an eighteenth-century parliamentary system. But I must tell you candidly that I do not believe it is possible to use the institutions devised by another class in another period to meet the needs of our people in this period. Yet Labour has dismissed all this as irrelevant – Jim Callaghan used to call it an 'arid constitutional wrangle' if ever you raised matters of institutions.

Then Labour has never tackled the media. Don't misunderstand me; I don't want to nationalise the media so they tell us what we should think, but the *Obscurer* and the *Weekly Chloroform* in Tressell's book are now much stronger than they were before the First World War. We have a virtual press monopoly and we saw the role of Murdoch behind his barbed wire in Wapping. Television and radio under the BBC and the IBA have replaced the old medieval Church. In medieval times there was a priest in every pulpit every Sunday who told you what God wanted you to do and what the King wanted you to do. Now we have a pundit on every channel every night who tells you there is no alternative to what Mrs Thatcher wants to do. The role of the BBC as a supplement and backer-up of this policy is now very apparent, and Labour leaders have not tackled it, although without fair media it is very hard to build up our movement.

The working class has had – and still has – a huge role to play in politics, from the campaign against the Combination Acts to the vote, the Labour Representation Committee, the Labour Party and Clause Four. The Establishment have always tried to divide the industrial from the political movement, to break the Trades and Labour Councils and to incorporate the trade union leaders into the National Economic Development Council and the Manpower Services Commission, and by using the honours list and the House of Lords. This has weakened the impact of working-class organisation on the political life of the nation. The labour movement has taken too narrow a view of the groups they should be representing. Women are not properly represented today in the trade unions or the Labour Party, nor are the black communities. Then there is the exclusion of the Greens and the failure to see quickly enough the importance of the environmental movement, All these factors have weakened the impact of the Labour Party in its role as the representative of working people.

Another failure has been the absence of moral appeal or vision. Politics seems to be all about competence, glamour, pollsters replacing the electors. Until we begin saying certain things are *right* and certain things are *wrong*, instead of *profitable* and *unprofitable*, you will never mobilise enough of the majority to make a change.

We must also think more deeply about the system of Parliamentary government which is saying to people, 'We will bring about transformation by proxy. Vote for us and we will do it for you.' Politics then becomes a spectator sport. You sit at home and watch the Eurovision Song Contest one night and a by-election the next night and the Oscar awards in Hollywood the third night and become separated from the process of political change. Parliamentarianism of this kind is usually accompanied by a great disapproval of extra-parliamentary activity.

Another obstacle to socialism is the theory that the working class has disappeared which is quite untrue and is one of the reasons why we haven't made more progress.

The last factor explaining our weakness is the absence of a strategy. If Labour wins the next election, there will be a run on the pound and a crisis of business confidence. Public expectations will be very high because people will be cheering in the streets and bonfires lit, countered by enormous pressure from capital to stop Labour from doing anything. How are we going to handle that situation? There is a desperate need for an informed public opinion that understands before you win what it is all about. History has shown that when capitalism gets into crisis it is more likely to go to the Right, unless you have an informed opinion, which is what gives the role of analysis, of teaching, such a lot of importance.

If you were to look at how the socialism of which Tressell wrote could be built, I think you have to go back to the importance of solidarity. When the miners are on strike, you support them; when the print workers are on strike, you support them; when Liverpool is attacked, you support Liverpool. You learn by experience because the discovery of talent during the miners' strike was phenomenal to see. I heard speeches made by miners and miners' wives which, frankly, had they been recorded and typed up, would have ranked with the greatest socialist orations in our history. If you asked them afterwards, they voted for Mrs Thatcher in 1983.

The basis of social change must be you do it yourself. In struggle, people get an education for which there is no substitute. We need a clear view of what we stand for. There are more socialists now than for fifty years and if you look abroad the international basis of class forces has shifted sharply against capital as a result of the anti-imperialist campaigns that have occurred since the war. We need to recreate an international of Labour to provide some counterbalance to the multinationals and the bankers.

We have tried in Chesterfield, in my own constituency, over the last year to set out our aims and objectives. We had a draft and discussed it in the Executive, sent it round to one thousand members of the Party. Every ward discussed it: ten of them had special meetings. Every trade union branch discussed it. We had two General Council meetings and about two whole Sundays on it, and I think about fifty amendments were moved and about 165 speeches were made and we published it. When I look at it now in the light of the responsibility you have put on my shoulders to give this lecture this afternoon, I am proud that out of the Chesterfield Labour Party and trade unions came something with which I think Tressell would have agreed. It begins:

> The Chesterfield Constituency Labour Party is a democratic, socialist and internationalist party with a growing membership made up of men and women, young and old, who are widely representative of all aspects of the life of the town closely linked to the trade unions and other affiliated organisations in pursuit of the historic role of Labour as a non-doctrinaire party of class struggle.

Then it goes on to talk about our beliefs: in certain rights of democracy and socialism, in internationalism, in self-determination, in solidarity, that conscience be above the law (long debate about that; some said if you put that out it will look as if you are in favour of anarchy, and then everyone got up and said, "Well, what have we been doing for the last year except fighting against the law in support of the miners?"), in the right of all to their beliefs, in progress through collective action, that we are servants of the community, and in more democracy.

Tressell's contribution to the reawakening of hope is that he gave us a torch to pass on from generation to generation. He gave us a lamp to light the way. He showed us that there is a light at the end of the tunnel. Robert Tressell is a teacher for our time who speaks from the past to give us hope for the future – and what more can anyone do but that!

Women and Socialism in Robert Tressell's World

Eileen Yeo

26 April 1987, Falaise Hall, Hastings

Today, I would like to look at women and socialism in Robert Tressell's world – and in our world. I hope it won't be too shocking to start by saying that Tressell's world seems largely to be a man's world. His novel, *The Ragged Trousered Philanthropists*, aims to paint 'a faithful picture of working-class life – more especially of those engaged in the Building trades' [Preface]. His masculine eye focuses sharply (but not entirely) on male wage-earners and their male employers, deeply entrenched in a state of industrial war. Moving beyond the novel into the world of the socialist and labour movements of his time, Tressell's views were typical and widespread. A close reading of his attitudes to women and socialism is helpful for exploring a wider socialist terrain and for spying out its open roads and high points as well as its barriers and pitfalls.

I would like to divide my talk this afternoon into three parts. First, I want to explore women in the world of Tressell's novel and point up some characteristic presences in the novel and some striking absences. Secondly, I want to look at women in the world of the socialist movement in Tressell's time. Here, I would like like to try to hear at least one woman talking in her own voice about her experience and her yearnings. Thirdly, I would like to look at women in the socialist world over a longer period, moving from the time of Robert Owen, through the time of Tressell's hero Frank Owen (any resemblance purely intentional!) to the world of socialism today.

Women in the World of *The Ragged Trousered Philanthropists*

Tressell's novel, as I have already noted, in mainly set in the male worlds of the workplace and public politics. Most of the chapters take us on the job as the decorating firm of Rushton and Company works to do up a house called the Cave for Mr Sweater. The realities and humiliations of employer's power are sharply etched: men taking underpriced work out of fear that their families will starve: men working relentlessly out of fear that they will be discovered slacking and given the sack by a sneaky, spying foreman aptly named Hunter; men never daring to object when their craftmanship is sacrificed or when safety itself is sold out to make profits for the boss (who is himself locked into competition with even more underpriced firms like Driver and Botchitt). Dinner-time provides a kind of literary space for the workmen to discuss their views on poverty, its causes and cure. They talk especially in reaction to lectures from the socialist Owen, who keeps his job because he is such a fine workman, and the socialist Barrington whose 'Great Oration' gives the fullest exposition of what socialism will be like.

Like a cancer, economic power grows into political might. The employers and owners are a mafia which also controls the local Council and use their power to line their own personal pockets. What scoundrels they are is immediately and sarcastically conveyed by their names and by chapter headings like 'The Forty Thieves', to describe a meeting of these pious local worthies. Mr Sweater, the Mayor, is not only a large slum landlord, but owns a big drapery business and manufactures garments, often using female labour at home to get the work done really cheap. Mr Amos Grinder, the grocer, makes a speciality of driving small traders out of business and exploiting his monopoly position. Mr Didlum takes advantage of the workers' necessity by buying their precious furniture cheap and selling it dear. And so on. Needless to say, these eminent citizens also control Liberal Party parliamentary bids, while the Tory interest is represented by a more established and venerated kind of thief, Sir Graball D'Encloseland, complete with the Frenchified name, the most recent incarnation of the Norman Yoke.

Despite the fact that much of the novel takes place in the male territory of waged work and electoral politics, the world of family and home where women feature is also important, both in the men's minds and in the construction of the book. Not only are the families very precious to the men and worth every sacrifice, but they are strategic to the men's sense of self and especially their idea of their own masculinity. The employers know that they can get the men to do almost anything by playing upon their fear of their relatives being harmed. The families are important in the structure of the novel because they most clearly convey the terrible effects of employer power, low wages and irregular work over the twelve month period that Tressell wants to explore. Each household disintegrates over the course of the year and particularly during the winter months when the men are laid off. Two families are kept more in the background: the Newmans, plunged into dire straits when the father is put in jail for non-payment of rates and the Whites, where the widowed mother struggles to launch her apprentice son Bert into independent adulthood.

Three families are spotlighted. Firstly, the Owens, composed of Frank Owen himself who suffers from tuberculosis, his wife Nora, also suffering from an unnamed disease and their bright but undernourished son Frankie. Winter takes its toll on all of them.

Although Owen is one of the last workmen to be 'slaughtered', or totally laid off, nonetheless he has less work. The result is that everyone's health deteriorates and one day Owen even finds his mouth full of blood.

The second family in focus are the Lindens where the usual insecurity is compounded by old age. Jack, aged 67, is fired when Rushton and Company want to make way for underpriced men. He can no longer find work and his whole household, composed of his aged wife, his widowed daughter-in-law Mary and her two children Charlie and Elsie, suffers and slowly falls apart. With Jack unemployed and his grown sons unwilling to help, the household comes to depend on Mary's earnings from machining blouses at home for Sweater. But this money is not enough and Mary starts selling all her furniture until virtually everything is gone. The rent in arrears, Sweater, who is also their landlord, gives them notice to quit. The old people go into the Workhouse leaving Mary and her children unprotected and demoralized. Mary, becoming indifferent to her crumbling and nearly denuded house, collapses and is discovered lying unconscious by her children. Finally, she is helped by Owen who suggests that she take the spare room at the house of the equally desperate Eastons and thereby have a roof over her head while she helps the other family to pay their rent.

The Eastons are the third family in the spotlight and they reveal most about Tressell's attitudes to relations between women and men. In the Easton household things go most grievously wrong, not only because of outside pressures beyond the family's control. But even worse, men refuse to play their proper roles and the husband especially will not face up to his responsibilities. What is the desired state of things is sometimes most clearly conveyed by its opposite, the most disastrous state of things. The ideal of a good marriage sometimes becomes most visible when it is most conspicuously transgressed. Will Easton, another of Rushton's workmen, marries Ruth, a servant, when she falls pregnant with baby Freddie. They set up a household with good intentions and good furnishing, including oilcloth on the floor and a three-piece suite bought second-hand or on hire-purchase.

But the first winter of their marriage and Will's first period of unemployment put an enormous strain on the family exchequer, disclosed in a chapter called 'The Financiers' which spells out the material pressures which underlie marital stress. Convinced that Ruth is not managing adequately, Will tries to teach her to suck eggs by making out a list of all their debts. He finds out not only that there are payments currently due, but also an accumulation of debts from other periods of unemployment which she is trying to pay off in a nimble balancing act, always juggling the least pressing bill to the back of the queue. As the nightmare of trying to manage on his earnings becomes clearer, he becomes more 'impatient' and irritable, and finally attacks her verbally:

> "...I think it's your part to attend to the house, but it seems to me you don't manage things properly." [**p 58**, p 57]

This is a most unfair blow because her self-esteem and her idea of femininity is tied up with being a good manager and she has made a remarkable job of it in the circumstances at considerable personal cost. One of her stratagems has been to starve herself, telling him that she has already eaten while he was out when in fact she has taken little or nothing. If anything she is being eaten up in two directions: her husband is taking food which should have been hers, while the baby is breast-feeding her dry. Feeling deflated and devalued, she weakly and silently weeps:

> She was wondering if he still thought she managed badly, and what he would do about it. She knew she had always done her best. At last she said, wistfully, trying hard to speak plainly for there seemed to be a lump in her throat: "And what about tomorrow? Would you like to spend the money yourself, or shall I manage as I've done before, or will you tell me what to do?"
>
> "I don't know, dear", said Easton, sheepishly, "I think you'd better do as you think best."
>
> "Oh, I'll manage all right, dear, you'll see," replied Ruth, who seemed to think it a sort of honour to be allowed to starve herself and to wear shabby clothes.[**p 62**, pp 60-61]

Will and Ruth decide to let their spare room as a way to make ends meet and they find a lodger, Will's workmate Slyme who, as his name suggests, is not the most savoury character despite his sanctimonious air. At first to keep in with the foreman, Will starts to go to the pub straight after work. When he finally comes home drunk, he presses himself upon Ruth in a revolting way:

> She shrank away, shuddering with involuntary disgust as he pressed his wet lips and filthy moustache upon her mouth.... He kissed her repeatedly and when at last he released her she hastily wiped her face with her handkerchief and shivered. [**p 206**, p 191]

Ruth becomes the quintessential defenceless victim. Mentally and physically assaulted and thrown off balance by her husband, she is left exposed to the advances of Slyme, who has been ingratiating himself by wooing the baby with sweets and toys. The chapter culminating in her rape is powerful melodrama, drawing on familiar conventions. For the first time in her life, Ruth is taken to a pub by her husband and feels 'dazed', 'bewildered', 'confused', 'ill at ease'. Unable to get him to come home, she determines to leave by herself, and he reacts savagely:

> "Well, go by yourself if you want to!" shouted Easton fiercely, pushing her away from him...Ruth staggered and nearly fell from the force of the push he gave her.... [**pp 263-4**, p 244]

She goes out into the dangerous city at night on her own and in this condition is unable to cope with the hurly-burly of life symbolized by the crush to get onto the public tram:

> ...then ensued a fierce struggle amongst the waiting crowd for the vacant seats. Men and women pushed, pulled and almost fought, shoving their fists and elbows into each other's sides and breasts and faces. Ruth was quickly thrust aside and nearly knocked down... [**p 264**, p 245]

Finally she is 'rescued' by Slyme on his way back from the open-air prayer meeting of the Shining Light Mission. He guides her home where he pounces on her, as he helps to remove her jacket:

> It took a very long time to get this jacket off, because whilst he was helping her, Slyme kissed her repeatedly and passionately as she lay limp and unresisting in his arms. [**p 267**, p 248]

Slyme does a bunk and winter draws on. Only the friendship of Mary Linden, who has moved into the spare room, and Nora Owen, her old school friend, keep Ruth from total despair. In due course, Ruth gives birth to an illegitimate child and tries to commit suicide by drowning herself in a lake in a park. Fortunately she can't find a way in because the park has recently been enclosed with railings. She decides instead to live independently of Will and moves in with the Owens. At the point where Will is feeling the discomfort of life without Ruth, Owen, who is Tressell's mouthpiece for the correct views on this marital matter, gives Will a full-frontal blast of the truth:

> "...you had a good wife and you ill-treated her... You may not have struck her, but you did worse – you treated her with indifference and exposed her to temptation. What has happened is the natural result of your neglect and want of care for her. The

> responsibility for what has happened is mainly yours, but apparently you wish to pose now as being very generous and to 'forgive her' – you're 'willing' to take her back; but it seems to me that it would be more fitting that you should ask her to forgive you." [**p 601**, p 557]

Finally, after Will makes his apology, he and Ruth are reconciled.

I now want to pull away from the narrative and pull out several points about Tressell's characterization of women which the stories illustrate and also to call attention to what has been missed out. Firstly, I feel that Tressell sees women as basically vulnerable and dependent. They are in need of protection from men and especially from husbands whose essential role is not only to provide a wage packet but also to safeguard them. Ruth is the most extreme case of fragility, with her sexuality representing her vunerability to greater power. Presenting Ruth in this way draws upon a long-standing tradition. During the whole of the nineteenth century, working men had represented class as well as personal exploitation in terms of a stronger party taking sexual advantage of the weaker. A powerful way to express class exploitation was to conjure up an image of class rape, the seduction of the innocent working-class women, first by the aristocrat and later by the capitalist employer. So, for example, in Chartist times, plug plot rioters made lurid suggestions about what went on while their women were left unguarded in the cotton mills and Chartists in a most chivalric language asserted their duty to protect the virtue of their womenfolk. Tressell draws upon the rape image to represent unwholesome personal relations, too.

But if Ruth is the most vulnerable, all of the women in the novel are portrayed as more or less exposed, languishing, collapsed or ill. They all depend on male support or rescue. Mrs. Newman, left in charge and desperate when Newman is jailed, is saved by Owen organising a whip-round of her husband's workmates. Apprentice Bert's widowed mother is helped by Owen who explodes at Rushton for refusing the boy a fire and threatens to report him to the NSPCC. Mary Linden collapses into unconsciousness and is rescued by Owen's suggestion that she move in with the Eastons. Nora Owen's weakness keeps her in a semi-reclining position for most of the novel from which she does her domestic work, with the help of young Frankie and of Owen who ignores his own tuberculosis to make it possible for her to get some rest. Her health is finally shattered by the significant fact that she goes outside her home to work in a boarding house. From the images of the danger that exists outside the home – the disorientating pub for Ruth, the scramble for the public streetcar, the health-destroying work for Nora – we get the idea that Tressell would prefer to keep his women protected at home.

Tressell's views were the common-sense in the labour movement at the time. Two ideals dominated: the domestic ideal, that a woman's place was in the home, and the ideal of a family wage, that the male breadwinner earn enough to support a dependent wife and children. Yet despite Tressell's commitment to the home, he does not focus women's *unpaid* family and domestic work. While there is the excellent account of Ruth's problems about managing the domestic economy, which was an essential part of women's work, there is little about other unpaid household or familial duties. We often come home after work with Tressell to find, in the good times anyway, a scrupulously clean and cosy house with a table set invitingly for tea. But the hardness of the physical labour of housework which produces this result is not detailed, especially the drudgery of doing laundry not only for the family but for outsiders to augment the family income. Think of drawing water from an outside tap, of boiling up huge cauldrons, of washing large amounts of clothing and sheets by hand, of humping the heavy, wet washing to a place to dry it – often the whole interior of the house. Then think of the problems of cooking, sometimes on an inefficient stove, but often over an open fire which could only hold one pot at a time. Then there were the family tasks – of giving birth to children and having the main responsibility for raising them. Often this involved an almost unending stream of pregnancies punctuated by fairly regular obstetric disasters. The women in *The Ragged Trousered Philanthropists* have at most two children. But in the first decade of the twentieth century, 55% of women had three or more children and 25% more than five: working-class women had much larger families than richer women.

When Barrington unwraps the socialist package, he says little that speaks to these areas of women's experience. He holds out the promise of a system where state employees will get good pay for drastically reduced hours of labour and where production will stock National Service Retail Stores which will supply 'the necessaries of life at the lowest possible prices'. It is not clear just who is to carry on working, but one reasonable guess is that Tressell had mind a male wage-earner making a family wage. And of course this arrangement would ease the strain on a married woman relying on her husband's wage to make ends meet. Probably, Tressell would also have included women who had to earn to maintain their independence, since his sharp eyes have already picked out the exploitative features of typical 'women's work' – Ruth's time as a domestic servant under the tyrannical Mrs. Starvem, Nora's health breaking when she goes out to char, Mary's fancy blouse work being paid at the same low rate as the simple work.

But there is no mention in Barrington's discourse of how the drudgery of housework or how the labour, in many senses, of childbirth and child-rearing is to be restructured under socialism. Perhaps it is silly to look for this in a workplace lecture spoken entirely to men. His one mention of afterwork activity does not really take the experience of women into account:

> At the age of forty-five, everyone will be allowed to retire from the State service on full pay.... All these will be able to spend the rest of their days according to their own inclinations: some will settle down quietly at home, and amuse themselves in the same way as people of wealth and leisure do at the present day – with some hobby, or by taking part in the organisation of social functions, such as balls, parties, entertainments, the organisation of Public Games and Athletic Tournaments, Races and all kinds of sports. [**p 521,** p 481-2]

What about women for whom the home is the location not only of rest but of some or their heaviest toil? If they are to be home-based, what are *their* chances for realizing *their* full humanity, for developing any potential they find in themselves? Suppose they don't wish to marry? Suppose they discover inclinations, even yearnings, which are not easily compatible with the domestic ideal?

Women in the World of the Socialist Movement in Tressell's Time

I am asking these questions not to carp at the past, but because socialist women in Tressell's time asked them. It is now the moment to move on to my second section and to listen to the voices of women who tell us about their experiences and their aspirations. Such voices are hard to find: working women are often the most silent of the silent majority as far as conventional historical sources are concerned, not least because their sphere was seen to be domestic, not the sphere of public life in which history was supposedly made.

Luckily for us, it was precisely in the late-nineteenth-century labour movement that some women felt the need to write and speak publicly. The Women's Co-operative Guild, founded in 1883, composed mainly of married women at home, aimed to open a life of active citizenship to its members, and give them the skills for public life which included the skills for running meetings and the skills for public speaking and writing. It also created space where they could speak their experience in their own voices, bringing their private worlds into the public arena with books like *Maternity: Letters From Working Women* [1915, reprinted by Virago Books, editor M L Davies, 1978] and later life stories collected into the book, *Life As We Have Known It* [Hogarth Press, London, 1931]. Researchers wanting to explore the sensibility of Mugsborough women in Tressell's time could begin by searching out the Hastings Guild branch which was started in 1914. Other sources for voices, individual autobiographies came out of the lively movements of the time (a tradition which is now being kept, alive and well, within people's history and within the Federation of Worker Writers and Community Publishers). Women wrote for the Socialist Press which also ran women's columns: Julia Dawson's in *The Clarion* and Lily Bell's in *Labour Leader* were perhaps the best known. From these many voices, I will select only one as a counterpoint to Tressell, that of Hannah Mitchell author of the autobiography, *The Hard Way Up* [Virago Books, 1984].

Born into rural poverty in Derbyshire in 1871, one of a family of six children, Hannah's early experiences of marriage and motherhood as lived by her parents were not ideal. The children weighed the mother down to the point where she would fly into wild rages which would send the father fleeing to the barn for shelter. From early on Hannah discovered in herself a passionate thirst for books and learning which as a poor girl she was never in a position to slake. She had only one week of formal schooling and picked up education higgledy-piggledy where she could, finding within the socialist movement her real university. It was in the Labour Church that she started speaking in public for the first time. Like many socialists of the period, what drew her into the movement was the promise of a wider and fuller life, a world of beauty and joy:

> The Labour Church attracted a type of Socialist who was not satisfied with the stark materialism of the Marxist school desiring warmth and colour in human lives: not just bread, but bread and roses, too. Perhaps we were not quite sound on economics as our Marxian friends took care to remind us, but we realized the injustice and ugliness of the present system. We had enough imagination to visualize the greater possibility for beauty and culture in a more justly ordered state. If our conception of Socialism owed more to Morris than to Marx, we were none the less sincere...[p 116]

As soon as possible she left home and, unable to bear domestic service (despising the 'muslin badge of servitude'), she got work as a needlewoman, sewing dresses and shirts (jobs well-known in Tressell's world). She probably would never have married had it not been for the fact that her fellow-lodger and sweetheart was a socialist and that socialists

> were talking of marriage as a comradeship, rather than a state where the woman was subservient to, and dependent on, the man.

> Limiting the population as a means of reducing poverty was one the new ideas, new to me anyhow. I soon came to believe as indeed I still do that although birth control may not be a perfect solution to social problems, it is the first and the simplest way at present for the poor to help themselves, and by far the surest way for women to obtain some measure of freedom. [pp 88-9]

For Mitchell, unlike Tressell, the question of women's independence was crucial and related issues of dependence upon men and of family size were central. The Women's Co-operative Guild was also very concerned with the tyranny of maternity and although they did not openly advocate birth control in the early years, they did call for more knowledge of physiology, for State money for maternity benefit and, even though this led to great ructions with the Co-operative men, easier divorce. All in the name of making motherhood more enjoyable and efficient.

After marriage, Hannah discovered that many people, even including socialists, did not practise what they preached:

> I soon found out that a lot of the Socialist talk about freedom was only talk and these Socialist young men expected Sunday dinners and huge teas with home-made cakes, potted meat and pies, exactly like their reactionary fellows....they believed in "freedom's cause" but thought that liberty is a kind of thing that "don't agree with wives". They expected that the girl who had shared their week-end cycling or rambling, summer games or winter dances, would change all her ways with her marriage ring and begin where their mothers left off. [p 96]

Hannah found the housework, and especially the cooking, to be fatal to ambition:

> Home life was in those days, indeed still is, for the wife and mother a constant round of wash days, cleaning days, cooking and serving meals. "The tyranny of meals" is the worst snag in the housewife's lot. Her life is bounded on the north by breakfast, south by dinner, east by tea, and on the west by supper, and the most sympathetic man can never be made to understand that meals do not come up through the tablecloth but have to be planned, bought and cooked. [pp 112-3]

Here then, we have a woman who is in a tradition which stretches right back to Mary Wollstonecraft and the French Revolution. She cherished independence and wanted a life of politics and of the mind. She repudiated the idea of woman as a dependent and found that socialism addressed problems of class but not of gender. Her husband, despite her trace of sour grapes, was in fact a good man, but he was caught in the very stereotype of masculinity and marriage that she found so limiting. He obviously agreed to their having only one child and he came out to serve as her bodyguard when she gave open-air suffragette talks around the Lancashire townships. But when it came to the domestic front, he just lost his way. When she landed in jail and was determined to stay there, he showed up, to her intense annoyance, to pay her fine. She remarked bitterly, 'most of us who were married found that "Votes for Women" were of less interest to our husbands than their own dinners' [p 149]. The fact that socialism did not seem to worry about gender stereotyping or women's toil seemed to her to undercut its promise.

Her way of resolving the conflict between her ambition and her situation was typical. Instead of being the doubly burdened wife, she became triply burdened taking responsibility first for the domestic and family duties, second for bringing extra income into the household through her sewing (and taking in lodgers) and third trying to have a public political life as well. Unlike male socialists, she problematized not only the politics of housework but the housework of politics. Who would do the housework and look after the family while she was out politicking? Not surprisingly it was family and neighbourhood networks of women who came to her aid, and the help did not only come from socialists. She has left this fascinating account of how she organised her day of work as a Poor Law Guardian, an office to which she was elected as an Independent Labour Party candidate:

> I could never have managed to do my work as Guardian had it not been for the help of a kindly neighbour whom I had the good fortune to meet soon after coming to Ashton in 1900....This friend, Mary Hartley, was a young wife with a little baby when I first met her. Later two more sons and a daughter arrived so she also had her hands full. She was not a Socialist although she possessed the breadth of mind and love of beauty which characterized the early Socialists. Although she herself was an excellent mother, a good cook, and a thoroughly capable housewife, she did not wish to force every woman into the kitchen, her own inclinations being rather to a business than to a domestic life.... when I became a Poor Law Guardian, she at once offered to cook the dinner when I attended the weekly Board meeting. This began at ten o'clock; it was followed by the Relief Committee; the Hospital Committee met in the afternoon. This

> made a full day's work. I would rise early, clean up, make beds and prepare the dinner which Mary cooked for me, and get to the Board meeting by ten o'clock. At eleven we went into Relief Committee until twelve thirty. Then I rushed home to serve the dinner, and often got back to Hospital Committee at two o'clock without having time for any food except a cup of tea and a biscuit. Our niece was a very clever and willing girl and soon learned to get the teas, and wash the dishes, as well as I could myself. I had also taught the boy (her son) to make himself useful, and as he too was willing, we got along fairly well. [pp 125-6]

But 'fairly well' must really have meant with a lot of difficulty. It is not surprising that many of these women socialists, while being passionately committed to a fairer distribution of wealth and power, were also interested in any contemporary movement which raised gender issues and questions of women's power. Yet this very kind of concern, about women's suffrage for instance, was hampered by the very problems of sexual politics that it sought to address. As Hannah put it, and I will give her the last word in this part of the talk:

> No cause can be won between dinner and tea, and most of us who were married had to work with one hand tied behind us, so to speak. Public disapproval could be faced and borne, but domestic unhappiness, the price many of us paid for our opinions and activities, was a very bitter thing. [p 130]

Women and Socialism from the Time of Robert Owen to Frank Owen to Our World

Hannah's yearnings and disappointments were not new. One hundred years before, when Robert Owen inspired the early socialist movement, women were expressing similar feelings. Although Marxists have dismissed Owenism as utopian and unscientific, the Owenite socialist movement, which flourished between 1825 and 1850, actually allowed more space for the consideration of power relations and of oppression in the family and between the sexes than did later socialisms. The Owenites asserted the equality of male and female nature and gave women rationality as part of their potential to develop. Some Owenites even felt sex tyranny to be as exploitative as wage slavery and identified household drudgery as the equivalent of man's toil. Within the movement, scientific ingenuity was applied to rationalizing and lightening housework and women talked about the need for 'nature's chastity' in socialist partnerships to limit family size. Of course these fine ideas did not always sit comfortably with actual practice in socialist homes or branches, where men often governed while women made the tea. In letters to the Woman's Page of the *Pioneer* newspaper in 1834, women sadly told of how their husbands opposed their attending union meetings and attacked them for being unfeminine or, in their language, 'unsexed'.

In many ways and for many reasons, by the time of Robert Tressell and Hannah Mitchell, ideas of femininity and masculinity had hardened, making it more difficult for working-class women to explore new gender possibilities. The role of the man as protector of his endangered family, which was common sense to Tressell, had been sanctified by the Chartists during the Owenite years. This was an understandable reaction to real problems but not perhaps the most creative. Capitalist employers were using women and children to undercut the industrial power of men and disrupting family patterns of authority into the bargain. The State, in the form of the New Poor Law and the Union Workhouse with its segregation by sex and age, threatened to destroy families altogether. The Rev. J.R. Stephens, the People's Minister and one of the fiercest opponents of the New Poor Law, was important in consecrating the protective element in true masculinity. He told his congregations composed of mill-workers and Chartists that women's essential nature had been revealed when God chose Mary to carry Jesus and act as the vessel of salvation. Since vessels were fragile, it was men's duty to protect their womenfolk. Certainly this was a more humane attitude than the Evangelical stance during the same years which started from the premise that Eve had tempted Adam in the Garden of Eden and that women deserved to be punished for this sin – even punished threefold. The idea that masculinity involved a defending role was reinforced by the family-wage demand which increasingly became part of trade union strategy from the mid-nineteenth century onward. By Tressell's and Mitchell's time, it had become dominant. Men were to earn enough to look after a dependent wife and children living at home where they could be safe.

Neither the formation of the Labour Party nor the experience of reconstruction after two World Wars did much to shift the ideal of the family wage from its position of dominance. After World War Two, women's part-time work in the public labour force became more acceptable and to an extent challenged the domestic ideal, or perhaps made it more burdensome since women were expected to do both paid public work and their unpaid domestic work as before. It was the resurgence of the women's movement of the 1970s which sent shock-waves through the socialist world which have not yet been stilled. Again, as many times before, women have set an agenda for socialism which contains several critical and rather familiar items.

First on the agenda, the need to examine sex stereotyping for both men and women. You can't have one without the other. It is a binary system. The idea of the protector male does not exist without the construct of the feeble female. More positively, this awareness of stereotypes can open the way to greater freedom for all of us to develop the potential we like in ourselves without being limited by false ideas of womanly or manly.

Second on the agenda, to be real for women, freedom needs to be underpinned by real material foundations. Socialist women have continuously been concerned with our need to control our own fertility. Owenite women praising 'nature's chastity', Hannah Mitchell talking of 'birth control' as 'the surest way for women to obtain some measure of freedom', women in the 1970s calling for 'free contraception' and 'abortion on demand' are all addressing the same issue.

Socialist women have also called for proper appreciation of the unpaid work which is often seen as woman's work, namely housework and childcare. In the 1970s, the demands for 24-hour nurseries and wages-for-housework were ways to call for a real recognition of the domestic role. Not only has the politics of housework been of concern, but the housework of politics. Who will look after the home and children to free women for any public activity if they want it? Now, in places like the Hastings WEA, creches come along with classes making it realistically possible for women to attend. Another material foundation considered important from at least Mary Wollstonecraft's time has been properly paid work (and more recently equal pay) to give the financial independence which is key to women's freedom.

Last on the agenda, the need to build on women's cultural strengths and to build with our experiences and voices. It is striking how mutual help networks have always been part of women's lives and cultivating them part of women's skills. These support networks are expressions of the deepest ethic and most central practice of socialism and should be valued and harnessed. Finally, and as part of all of these, space must be made for women to speak in their own voices. Just as no radical working man would have tolerated the idea that a richer man could represent him, so socialism must make the room for all sorts and conditions of human beings to speak for themselves. Socialists must be careful not to reproduce the idea of the *femme couverte*, the invisible woman, all over again, veiled behind the primacy of the class struggle.

An early socialist text, published in 1825, was called *Appeal of One Half of the Human Race, Women, Against the Pretensions of the Other Half, Men, to Retain them in Political, and thence in Civil and Domestic Slavery*. [by William Thompson, reprinted by Virago Books, 1983] But it was written by a man. The struggle was there in Robert Owen's time and continued into Frank Owen's time. We need to continue the struggle today to make certain that socialism keeps a promise which will free into new life not only half, but the whole of the human race.

Tressell and the Truths of Fiction

Bernard Sharratt

30 April 1988, Queens Hotel, Hastings

Let me begin with what may appear to be a detour. My subject is 'Tressell and the truths of fiction' – but for me that title has a silent question-mark at the end of it, a note of query about the very idea of fiction having or offering 'truths'. My initial detour will attempt to explain why.

In his own Tressell Memorial Lecture, in 1982, Raymond Williams, explaining his retitling of the book as *The Ragged-Arsed Philanthropists*, said this:

> I have a sore point about the title because I was prevented, for many years, from reading this extraordinary book in its then reduced edition, because I took it, from knowledge of its title alone, to be one of those maudlin Victorian tracts which showed that it didn't matter how poor you were, you could always help others, and I'd assumed – I suppose I shouldn't have – that it would be a sentimental tale of people down on their luck who were helping others...

I begin with Williams' admission about how long it took him to get over that title and actually read the book partly because my own talk is meant to be a kind of memorial for Raymond Williams as well as for Tressell; much of what I want to say will be in various ways indebted to Williams. And partly because I have an even more damaging admission to make: that I was put off for a very long time from reading *The Ragged Trousered Philanthropists* not just because of its title but simply because it was a novel. It wasn't in fact until after I'd seen a dramatic adaptation of the novel, by the Joint Stock Theatre Company in 1978, that I finally opened the book, though I'd bought a copy several years before. Since I assume that most of you will probably have read and re-read this novel that we are here to celebrate, you may well feel that my long reluctance to read it at all makes me an inappropriate memorialist.

But my reluctance wasn't, as I say, due to any specific prejudice against Tressell but to a general prejudice against the very form of the novel – an odd prejudice for somebody who, after all, teaches English – but one not untypical of my 'generation'. My detour is to attempt to explain that prejudice by offering a brief contrast between Raymond Williams' generation and my own.

Williams was born in 1921. His formative political moments were, arguably, the 1926 General Strike (in retrospect, that is – he was only five at the time!), the years of the depression, of Spain and the anti-Fascist struggle, of the Communist Party in the late 1930s, the War, and, crucially, the post-war Labour Government. Throughout those various moments, there was a strong, even overwhelming sense that the obvious and only place for a British socialist (in his case a Welsh socialist) was in the labour movement. Not necessarily, of course, in the Labour Party, but in some direct association and involvement with the organised working-class of this country. It was then an obvious route for him, on leaving Cambridge in 1946 or so, to take a job with the Oxford Delegacy, teaching in what was essentially a Workers' Educational Association context, based here in Hastings. Some of you, I hope, will remember him from those days. In 1961 he was transplanted back to Cambridge, with several books already written of what was to become the most impressive and wide-ranging body of socialist writing produced by any individual in this country since, probably, William Morris. And throughout those years and later Williams was not only teaching and writing about novels but actually writing novels.

My own formation, twenty years later, was different. I was born in 1944, simultaneously with the Education Act which eventually enabled me – as a Liverpool working-class kid – to end up in Cambridge in the 1960s, where I first met Raymond Williams. I graduated in 1968 – that turbulent year of the Paris 'Events' that is itself being so generally memorialised at present. On 1st May 1968, twenty years ago tomorrow, I was not, however, in Paris but at a launch meeting for the *May Day Manifesto*, edited by Williams. It was, nevertheless, that complex of events labelled "May '68" which was my decisive political formation and which indirectly – to come back to where we started – made me almost indifferent, for quite some time, to the reading of novels, including *The Ragged Trousered Philanthropists*. Yet I was, as a student, officially 'reading English'. Why the indifference? And what possible connection was there?

It's worth, I think, taking you on this brief detour through my life, because there's a large political and cultural issue lurking, to do with some still-active discontinuities between a kind of politics that in important respects could link Tressell and Williams and the political perspectives of that 1968 generation.

Let me put it this way. I did some research, on working-class autobiographies in the nineteenth century, but when I finally left Cambridge in 1971 I had three possible jobs or futures to choose between. One was a WEA job, in the Colne Valley or perhaps in Liverpool. I had put in for both posts and maybe would have had a chance of getting one. Second was an invitation to join a team in Central

America, based in Guatemala, working with peasant organisations and, eventually, with various liberation struggles, including the Sandinistas in Nicaragua. Third was a possible job teaching English at the then fairly new University of Kent.

For me, the real choice was between the second and third options. The first – the WEA job in a traditional working-class territory, in close association, probably, with a local labour movement and Labour Party organisation – seemed, at the time, a kind of anachronism, no longer where a socialist politics was to be located. That wasn't just, I think, the arrogance of youth nor simply the anger at what, under Wilson, the 'labour movement' had seemed to accept and even endorse: the acquiescence in American aggression in Vietnam, the failure to support African struggles against Smith and South Africa, the acceptance of an IMF view of the world, etc. The question could be put in this form: what, any longer, did the world of *The Ragged Trousered Philanthropists* have to say to me, a student socialist of '68, and why was I so unconcerned even to find out if it might have something to say? Part of the answer lies in the the notion of the 'truths' of fiction.

In May 1968 there appeared an essay which was to be very influential upon people of my formation and situation. It was an immensely ambitious essay, entitled 'Components of the National Culture', written by Perry Anderson, then editor of *New Left Review*. It tried to survey the whole range of British intellectual culture and to see why it operated as a block, as a stifling constraint upon the possiblity of socialism in this country. It's a difficult essay to quote briefly from so I'll try and paraphrase parts of its argument. [*New Left Review*, No. 50; reprinted in *Student Power*, edited by Alexander Cockburn and Robin Blackburn, Penguin Books, 1969]

In looking across the entire range of academic disciplines – history, philosophy, political studies, economics, anthropology, etc. – Anderson asked what characterised them, taken together, as the British intellectual culture. What he deliberately left out of his survey was any treatment of, on the one hand, literature, fiction, novels, and on the other the natural sciences. The grounds for this omission were that it was the area in between, the disciplines of the *social* sciences, which gave us the very concepts by which we can think adequately about the world we live in. What fiction gave was not concepts at all, and what the natural sciences dealt with was not the human world we construct and live in but the world of physics, of nature.

If we look at those disciplines which should give us the means to understand that human world what we find in England is a systematic refusal to think about the *whole* society. Each of those disciplines, those intellectual inquiries, took one fragment and deliberately refused to explore the connections with the other fragments: history had little to do with philosophy, economics ignored political theory, aesthetics was blind to economics, etc. What we needed, argued the essay, was a 'totalising' theory, a theory of society which tried to take on board the totality of where we live, all its aspects together. What in other intellectual traditions – in France, Germany, Italy – had provided that totalising theory was either Marxism or classical sociology, and that is precisely what British culture at its formal intellectual level excluded.

Instead, a curious gap or distortion appeared in that cultural terrain. What was trying to take the place of Marxism or sociology, what was trying to offer a kind of centre, a point from which the whole might be seen, was – of all things – literary criticism: the study of literature, of fictions. Anderson ended by pointing out that it wasn't then accidental that the leading socialist thinker of his generation, Raymond Williams, had himself developed out of literary criticism. If there was one place in the English cultural scene where some attempt to see the whole had actually taken place, it was literary criticism – though it shouldn't have been.

But why couldn't literature, the writing and reading of novels, provide the centre of the intellectual culture? After all, hadn't the great nineteenth-century novels sought, precisely, to embrace the whole society, to offer a 'total' account? What else is *Middlemarch*? But Anderson argued, against this, that after the emergence of Marxism and of Freudian psychoanalysis we now had radically new ways of understanding ourselves, but as yet those ways of understanding had not become naturalised and familiar to us. Nobody in ordinary life actually talks in Marxist or Freudian terms; their crucial analytical terms remain technical vocabularies. Those concepts which are central to the revolutionising of the way in which the twentieth century understands economy, family, power, society, have not yet been assimilated into the way we ordinarily talk about men and women, work and home. But since the novel rests upon and uses as its most basic material our ordinary language, until people begin to speak in conceptually adequate ways about their society no adequate post-Marx, post-Freud novel can be written.

Now, compare that case about the novel with the first critical book on Robert Tressell, which was published the following year, 1969: *Robert Tressell and the Ragged Trousered Philanthropists* by Jack Mitchell (with a foreword by, of course, Raymond Williams!). At one point Mitchell is talking about the Chartists' attempts to write socialist novels in the nineteenth century. What went wrong with those attempts, he says, was that they started from 'ideas', and a novel which starts from ideas and then tries, as it were, to dress them up in some form of story, is going to fail as a novel. Where you have to start from, for Jack Mitchell, and what he partly admires Tressell for, is with an absorbing curiosity about the men and women involved in struggle. If the 'artistic framework' is invented simply to illustrate a message, an idea, a concept, the book will fail as a novel. (p 31) Mitchell also claims that when you are reading a good novel, including Tressell's book, you 'cease to look upon what is happening as a story set in the past; [the reader] becomes involved in the action going on before his eyes as he would in something *unfinished*, something contemporary to him in his own life.' (p 67) And for Mitchell one of Tressell's merits is that his 'narrative prose is plain, sober, concrete – a clear glass, or rather lens, through which the reader views reality.' (p 64)

Now, each of these positions offered by Mitchell – the involvement in the story as real, the prose as a clear glass, fiction as being dependent not on ideas but on curiosity about people – I would have rejected at that time, for reasons which have political as well as literary or critical importance. Yet Mitchell's way of talking about novels does, in England, seem the 'obvious' way to think of 'reading a novel'. There is, in fact, a basic divergence here, not only between two moments or positions within the culture but also between two kinds of politics.

What followed from Anderson's analysis was the need for totalising concepts, for an overall theory which could build upon and bring together the new languages of Marx and Freud, as a basis for grasping, understanding, and thereby beginning to change, the *whole* of society. The basic political contrast here was, of course, with the deeply 'pragmatic' and 'commonsensical' approach of the leaders of the Labour Party and of most trades unions – in other words, a profound refusal to think about the *interrelations* between, say, wage demands and foreign policy, racism and exports, sexism and unemployment, media ownership and inflation, nuclear weapons and education. Each of these, in the perspective of conventional British politics, was only to be 'tackled' in terms of an essentially short-term and incremental approach, a matter of marginal reform, of single issue campaigns. The contrast with the total social change of the various Third World revolutions, or with the scope of the original Marxist project, or with the ambitious overall analysis of the *May Day Manifesto*, was clear. In the wake of Anderson's argument, and his editorial policy at *New Left Review*, therefore, a whole generation of British socialist intellectuals spent nearly a decade trying to arrive at (or simply import from Continental thinkers) such totalising concepts and theories. It was an extraordinary period, looking back, and it helped to confirm a fissure between two sides of what could have been one movement.

One of the ambitions of that period, among many of my contemporaries, was to arrive not only at a theory of the social totality but specifically at a *theory* of literature – a theory in which the 'commonsensical' attitude to literature was itself seen as something to be guarded against, as a dangerous fiction, and in which Jack Mitchell's way of reading was seen as collusive with those dangers. What was needed, as with any other area of social practice, was to analyse, to dismantle, the literary text, not to believe in its reality; to understand a fiction as a construction of effects, not to respond to it as 'a gallery of memorable characters'.

Let me try to illustrate the argument of that perspective by analysing the text of *The Ragged Trousered Philanthropists* itself. First, Tressell's own Preface to the book. He very firmly makes Mitchell's kind of distinction:

> ...'The Philanthropists' is not a treatise or essay, but a novel. My main object was to write a readable story full of human interest and based upon the happenings of everyday life, the subject of Socialism being treated incidentally.
>
> This was the task I set myself. To what extent I have succeeded is for others to say; but whatever their verdict, the work possesses at least one merit – that of being true. I have invented nothing. There are no scenes or incidents in the story that I have not either witnessed myself or had conclusive evidence of.

For Tressell here it seems that the 'truth' of fiction lies in his not having invented anything – in other words in it not being fiction, made up, at all. Yet he wants to insist that it's a novel, a story, not an essay or treatise. What this almost-contradictory claim invites, within the perspective of a theory of literature, is an analysis of *how* the *effect* of 'truth' might be created by a novel, by the writing in that novel operating not as a 'clear glass' but as a dense mesh of deliberate devices, each achieving a local but also cumulative *effect* of 'truth' and in so doing eliding that very distinction, and strain, between truth and invention.

If we now look at the first chapter of Tressell's novel we can see how he used some of the standard devices of novelists to give that effect of truth. Here's the first paragraph:

> The house was named 'The Cave'. It was a large old-fashioned three-storied building standing in about an acre of ground, and situated about a mile outside the town of Mugsborough. It stood back nearly two hundred yards from the main road and was reached by means of a by-road or lane, on each side of which was a hedge formed of hawthorn trees and blackberry bushes. This house had been unoccupied for many years and it was now being

> altered and renovated for its new owner by the firm of Rushton & Co. Builders and Decorators. [**p 13**, p 15]

A standard kind of opening. You describe something in exactly the way you would describe it if it were really in front of you. There is (almost) no trace here that this is fiction – and that is itself the deepest convention of the dominant form of the novel: to avoid awareness that what is described is not there to be described at all. But there are less obvious devices we can pick out from that first chapter. Take this sentence about one of the men trying to read what Tressell calls the *Obscurer*:

> Easton ... proceeded to laboriously work through some carefully cooked statistics relating to Free Trade and Protection. [**p 17**, p 19]

Compare the way those two qualifying phrases are used: 'laboriously' and 'carefully cooked'. You might take 'laboriously' as operating like the opening description, just telling us something that we could all agree on if we were actually there, watching this man: that he is having some difficulty reading the paper. But the other phrase, 'carefully cooked', clearly tells us something over and above a neutral 'description'. This is not something we would know just from looking at the newspaper. We're given an attitude, an opinion, alongside the statement that he is reading statistics; the opinion is the author's or narrator's and since we, as readers, are not ourselves given any access to those statistics, to judge for ourselves, we're in no position to challenge the claim that they are 'cooked': we just have to take it that they are. But, of course, 'laboriously' is not a neutral description either: it, too, when we think about it, is just as 'carefully cooked' as those alleged statistics.

Another device gives us a less blatantly direct impression of a 'truth'. We're given a description of a number of men, sitting down, in the middle of a working day, to have a cup of tea. We've been told earlier in the chapter that the place where they have their tea is surrounded by jam jars, broken cups, bits and pieces of crockery which are lying around in the dirt of the kitchen which is also used as the temporary paint-shop. Then we get this sentence:

> Another who took no part in the syndicate was Barrington, a labourer, who, having finished his dinner, placed the cup he brought for his tea back into his dinner basket and having closed and placed it on the mantelshelf above, took out an old briar pipe which he slowly filled, and proceeded to smoke in silence. [**p 17**, p 19]

We may not consciously notice the detail as we read, but if we do we are being prompted to ask why this man is so singled out, in not using one of the jam jars but a cup, and not a broken or dirty cup but a clean one he has brought with him. Those who have read the novel will know that this detail tells us a lot, retrospectively, about Barrington. But at this point in the novel the detail prompts a question to which we are not given the answer by the voice that is telling us the story. We spot the detail, but are not quite sure what to make of it.

Another device. The men get to talking about the house they are working on, with its odd name, which had after all been in the first sentence of the novel: 'The Cave'. On page 20 [**p 18**] we get:

> "Funny name to call a 'ouse, ain't it?" he said. " 'The Cave'. I wonder what made 'em give it a name like that."
>
> "They calls 'em all sorts of outlandish names nowadays," said old Jack Linden.
>
> "There's generally some sort of meaning to it, though," observed Payne.

We're not actually told here what the point of calling the house 'The Cave' is, but it's made pretty plain that the reader is being invited to think about why Tressell called it that.

What I'm trying to illustrate is the various ways in which, in these opening pages, the author, as any author does, uses a variety of devices through which, as we read, we become 'involved' in the story. We begin to learn things, to take them for granted – but we can also be pulled up short and asked to think about them. And we can then be told, or not told, what we are *supposed* to think about them. We can also be given 'exercises', in trying to work out whether what we are being told is the 'truth' or not. For instance, at one point, Owen, who is to become the spokesperson for one attitude towards socialism, is listening to a conversation among the other men arising out of something in the newspaper. We get this sentence:

> Owen was listening to this pitiable farrago with feelings of contempt and wonder. Were they all hopelessly stupid? Had their intelligence never developed beyond the childhood stage? Or was he mad himself? [**p 25**, p 27]

When we read that phrase, 'this pitiable farrago', are we to take it as what Tressell thinks of the conversation or only of what Owen thinks? Are we being invited to judge whether we agree with Owen here, or are we simply being told that it *was* a pitiable farrago (whether we think so or not)?

The last device I'll briefly comment on comes towards the end of the chapter, when there's an angry exchange in which Owen tries to explain why the people working on the house are in some ways worse off than slaves. He gets this response from one of the older workers:

> "Oh, I don't see that," roughly interrupted old Linden, who had been listening with evident anger and impatience. "You can speak for yourself, but I can tell yer I don't put *myself* down as a slave."
>
> "Nor me neither," said Crass sturdily. "Let them call their selves slaves as wants to."

The text goes on:

> At this moment a footstep was heard in the passage leading to the kitchen. Old Misery! or perhaps the Bloke himself! Crass hurriedly pulled out his watch.
>
> "Jesus Christ!" he gasped. "It's four minutes past one!" [**pp 29-30**, p 31]

Obviously, the author has so arranged the action that it confirms the 'truth' of one of the positions in the argument and undermines the other.

These, then, are among the standard devices of the novelist, deployed by Tressell in those opening pages. There are two basic strategies at work, and they constitute both the strength of the traditional novel and, I think, its dangers. Yet, interestingly, both these strategies are themselves questioned within this very chapter. Notice the earlier argument, about what is meant by 'poverty', in which we get this exchange:

> "Let us begin at the beginning," continued Owen, taking no notice of these interruptions. "First of all, what do you mean by Poverty?"
>
> "Why, if you've got no money, of course," said Crass impatiently.
>
> The others laughed disdainfully. It seemed to them such a foolish question.
>
> "Well, that's true enough as far as it goes," returned Owen, "that is, as things are arranged in the world at present. But money itself is not wealth: it's of no use whatever."
>
> At this there was another outburst of jeering laughter.
>
> "Supposing for example that you and Harlow were shipwrecked on a desolate island, and you had saved nothing from

the wreck but a bag containing a thousand sovereigns, and he had a tin of biscuits and a bottle of water."

"Make it beer!" cried Harlow appealingly.

"Who would be the richer man, you or Harlow?"

"But then you see we ain't shipwrecked on no dissolute island at all," sneered Crass. "That's the worst of your arguments. You can't never get very far without supposing some bloody ridiclus thing or other. Never mind about supposing things wot ain't true; let's 'ave facts and common sense." [**p 28**, p 29]

The passage speaks a lot to me because as a student I would get into rows with my Dad about politics or whatever, and say "Look, suppose..." and he'd say "Forget suppose!" But isn't the novelist essentially *supposing*? Let us suppose there is a house called 'The Cave'; let us suppose there are these men working in it; let us suppose they said this and did this. But when Owen tries that tactic himself within the novel, he's told he can't get anywhere in an argument by reaching for supposes. So how can the novel get anywhere by supposing?

The first basic strategy for the novelist, and basic problem for the reader, is that the novelist can suppose any 'bloody ridiclus thing' he likes (he can make it water or beer, a desolate or a dissolute island, as he wishes), but we can't as readers. We're dealing with someone else's made up fictions and we can't offer some counter-supposition in such a way that it has any effect whatsoever on the rest of the novel. We can exercise our judgement, we can decide for ourselves whether this clean cup or this desire for beer tells us something significant about a character or not – but we don't know whether it makes any difference which way we decide until we find out somewhere else in the novel that the author thinks it does too.

The second basic strategy is a kind of hierarchy, a setting of levels of authority and 'truth'. The text says something like 'Owen said X', but then we're told that 'Owen really thought Y'. We may then get a further level of comment, from the narrator: 'But what Owen didn't know was Z.' This is a characteristic pattern in many novels: a hierarchy of truth levels. 'This is true; but this is more true; and this is even more true.' Again, this chapter illustrates, and undermines, that pattern very well at one point:

"Well, I don't go in for politics much, either, but if what's in this 'ere paper is true, it seems to me as we oughter take some interest in it, when the country is being ruined by foreigners."

Notice that the issue is one of 'truth', and an appeal to what's printed, as an authority. But another voice cuts across:

> "If you're goin' to believe all that's in that bloody rag you'll want some salt," said Harlow.

And then a comment from the narrator:

> The *Obscurer* was a Tory paper and Harlow was a member of the local Liberal club. Harlow's remark roused Crass.

We are clearly to take the description of the paper as itself a true description, but also as affecting the truth of the paper's own claims. The text continues:

> "Wot's the use of talkin' like that?" he said, "you know very well that the country *is* being ruined by foreigners .... and I say it's about time it was stopped."
>
> "'ear, 'ear," said Linden, who always agreed with Crass, because the latter, being in charge of the job, had it in his power to put in a good – or a bad – word for a man to the boss. "'Ear, 'ear! Now that's wot I call common sense."
>
> Several other men, for the same reason as Linden, echoed Crass's sentiments... [**p 20**, p 22]

The pattern is clear here: we are told a statement claiming to be true, but then told the (true) reasons why those who assert it hold it to be true – because it agrees with their politics, or because the man who said it is powerful, or because it looks like 'common sense'. But the basis for the claim in the first instance was what was printed in a newspaper – and that paper, we are told, was 'a Tory paper' and (we have been told earlier) prints 'carefully cooked statistics'. But then the text goes on: 'but Owen laughed contemptuously.' It is, it seems, possible to oppose and even to laugh at these 'truths' of 'common sense' and Tory papers. But on what basis? By relying upon something printed in a different source, a different newspaper? Or in a novel perhaps? But what is the basis for any claims to truth of a novel?

I want to suggest that these basic strategies and various devices are what give us the impression of certain kinds of 'truth' within a novel, but since those devices have been developed within the classical bourgeois novel they raise for me certain problems about any attempt to write a 'working class' novel. At the core of the problem is a relationship between truth and fiction, and even though a novel can indeed put into question its own truth or its own status as fiction, in the end what the very form of a novel seems to resort to is the essential tactic of so arranging a hierarchy of truths within it that some of those truths are confirmed and some are disconfirmed by what 'happens' in the novel –

but what happens is what the novelist supposes to happen. Well, what danger is there in that? And why should it concern socialists anyway? And what's this got to do with a difference between traditional working class politics and what the post-68 generation detoured into? Let's pursue it a bit further.

Let's suppose we are on a desolate island, says Owen. In one sense that's where (we tend to suppose) the English novel started – with Defoe supposing about a desert island, in *Robinson Crusoe*. So let me sketch, very briefly indeed, some moments in the history of this curious relation between truth and fictions, in the development of the novel. Here's part of what Defoe says in his Preface to *Robinson Crusoe* (1719):

> If ever the story of any private man's adventures in the world were worth making public, and were accceptable when published, the editor of this account thinks this will be so.
>
> The wonders of this man's life exceeds all that (he thinks) is to be found extant; the life of one man being scarce capable of a greater variety.
>
> The story is told with modesty, with seriousness, and with a religious application of events to the uses to which wise men always apply them (viz.) to the instruction of others by this example, and to justify and honour the wisdom of Providence in all the variety of our circumstances, let them happen how they will.
>
> The editor believes the thing to be a just history of fact; neither is there any appearance of fiction in it

Defoe claims that this is a history of fact, that he is only the editor of a true story, one that really happened – and the extraordinary wonders that actually happened reveal, and instruct the reader in, the workings of Providence. Now, clearly, if I want to claim that a story shows the workings of Providence I can't admit that it's a story I simply made up; conversely, if I admit that the wonders are pure fiction they can hardly be used as evidence for Providence. But Defoe is actually engaged in a double move, both in the assertion of Providence and in a scientific repudiation of the need for miraculous explanations of how the world works, and this complicates the overall relation between truth and fiction.

At one point in the novel Crusoe finds with utter astonishment that corn is growing in his compound, though he hasn't planted any. This must, he thinks, be the action of God, 'the pure production of Providence for my support', and he gives heartfelt thanks to God. But then he remembers something: 'at last it occurred to my thoughts that I had shook a bag of chickens' meat out in that place, and then the wonder began to cease'. He thinks he has found a perfectly rational explanation so stops attributing the corn to Providence. But then, in a further twist, he thinks that perhaps it was indeed Providence which ensured that there should be a few grains at the bottom of the sack, that the divine has been working in 'scientific' ways – and again he thanks God. It's a classic moment of oscillation between two world-views, two entire explanatory schemas. But what Crusoe's final compromise position excludes, or suppresses, is the awareness that it wasn't God who arranged these events at all; it was Daniel Defoe, who devised the whole incident in the first place and who deliberately offers his readers two alternative explanations of what happened. Yet, fundamentally, Defoe represents himself as not in control at all; as only the editor of a true story.

By the time we get to Fielding's *Tom Jones* (1749), a generation later, Fielding is quite happy to admit that he is offering fiction. Indeed he cheerfully claims that since he's inventing this new way of writing, called the novel, he can therefore make up what rules he likes. The reader is entirely under his control, but it's for the reader's own good. Fielding will intervene occasionally, not only to arrange the events of the story, but to tell the reader what really happened, despite any misleading appearances. The reader will gradually become attuned to the rules of the genre and will finally learn to make his or her own judgements in accordance with those rules – and therefore, of course, in basic agreement with Fielding's own judgements, which, necessarily, constitute the 'truth' in the world of this fiction.

Some twenty years later, Horace Walpole, the son of Fielding's great political enemy, wrote *The Castle of Otranto*, initiating the vogue for the 'Gothic' novel. In the preface to the first edition he claims, like Defoe, to be only editing a manuscript he has found; but he leaves it peculiarly vague whether the manuscript is a true story or a fiction. He claims, with a great deal of circumstantial detail, that it is several hundred years old; but suggests that it was probably written by a priest who wanted to delude people into believing false supersitions; and then concludes: 'I cannot but believe that the groundwork of the story is founded on truth.' Then in the preface to the second edition, a few years later, he finally admits that he made up the story – but then claims that since he has observed the correct rules for writing fictions which have the authority of the great writers of the past, he is indeed offering a kind of truth.

A generation or so later, Jane Austen makes fun of the very conventions of the Gothic which Walpole relied upon, and even has an ironic glance at Defoe's notions of Providence. In *Persuasion* (1818) we have a blatantly engineered bit of plot coincidence, followed by the comment:

> "Putting all these very extraordinary circumstances together," said Captin Wentworth, "we must consider it to be the arrangement of Providence, that you should not be introduced to your cousin." (ch. 12)

Austen's own title for that novel indicates where the development of the novel has gone. It is concerned with the role and responsibility of persuasion (not scientific proof or religious belief) in society, and it also sets out itself to persuade the reader. It does so primarily by so constructing events and the fates of characters as to show the reader that they should have been persuaded this way rather than that. The final chapter opens:

> Who can be in doubt of what followed? When any two young people take it into their heads to marry, they are pretty sure by perseverance to carry their point, be they ever so poor, or ever so imprudent, or ever so little likely to be necessary to each other's ultimate comfort. This may be bad morality to conclude with, but I believe it to be truth. (ch. 24)

Indeed, yes, we might say. By the end of a Jane Austen novel who can be in doubt about the ending: we know who is bound to marry whom and who is going to be happy and unhappy. But what this claim has to exclude is the fact that in this novel, for example, there was indeed an alternative ending, an ending which Austen wrote and then rejected. And it was open to her to write whatever ending she pleased. The way the novel ends is offered as our basic validation for what we ought to believe about these characters. But what we are encouraged to forget is that how the novel ends is already built into what the author expects us to believe about those characters. It is not, after all, morality which governs the events, nor truth which decides them, but the author's capacity to persuade us to accept her morality as truth.

It would be possible to track this development further and in more detail. But let me suggest that its apotheosis has been in the dominant forms of film and television. As film took over certain of the functions of the novel in the early part of this century, what it perfected was a structure of presentation in which we literally 'see' the apparent truth of certain claims made within the film – and what the dominant form of the fiction film goes out of its way to avoid us realising is that the film itself is entirely constructed, that its effect of the real is indeed, in a new sense, a matter of editing. The same case can be made about much television, including the 'non-fiction' of the News: we are persuaded of the truth of that news by the apparent match between commentary and visual presentation, as in the nightly bulletins at present on the Dover seamen's struggle. But of course what we see, what has been edited for us to see, has been selected precisely to endorse what we are being told in the commentary.

Yet at precisely the point at which film narrative emerges out of the conventions of melodrama and the novel, the novel itself begins to bifurcate, to split into a continued traditional mode and a break with that dominant form, into what we call modernism. (As it happens, James Joyce, the great exemplar of how the novel finally breaks with the received bourgeois forms, once toyed with the idea of running his own cinema. It's one of several things he shares with his compatriot Robert Tressell/Noonan.) The crucial move in modernist fiction was to insist upon its own fictiveness, to leave the reader in no doubt that he or she was reading a constructed text, to make its devices visible. And at the same time to refuse any simple match between narrative authority, what happens, and what judgements the reader is to arrive at about what happens. In that development the relation between truth and fiction becomes itself part of the play of the fiction, as it had been in, say, Cervantes or Sterne. Let me close this sketch of the novel's history with the two prefatory comments in Robbe-Grillet's *The House of Assignation*

> The author wishes to make it clear that this novel is in no way intended to be an account of life in the British territory of Hong Kong. Any resemblance, in setting or situation, between the two is a matter of pure coincidence, whether objective or otherwise.

And, on the next page:

> Should any reader, knowing his Far-Eastern ports well, form the opinion that the places described here do not correspond to reality, the author, who has himself spent the greater part of his life there, would advise him to go back and look again: things change quickly in those parts.

It's time to summarise the argument thus far. Given those basic strategies, those various devices, and that fundamental relation between truth and fiction in the dominant form of the novel, there is – I want to suggest – a basic danger involved in the use of the form. Whatever the content of the novel, whatever its ideas, and whatever the reader's attitude to that content, in reading a novel constructed upon such devices we are being attuned, trained, inculcated, at the level precisely of our 'involvement', into accepting two basic procedures. One is to 'believe our betters' (to use a phrase from Tressell), that is, to take part in the construction of a hierarchy of truths in which some other person (the author, the narrator) not only is in control of what is happening but also claims to know the truth of what is happening – while we are left, in effect, having to believe what we're told. It's as simple, as basic, and in one sense as harmless as that; but as a structure of our relation to truth and control it's far from harmless, and it is arguably that very structure which is constantly and effectively offered to us as the most fundamental model of the society we actually inhabit, not just in the fictional world of the novel but in the world the novel claims to match, to represent. Think of this passage from Tressell:

> From their infancy they had been trained to distrust their own intelligence, and to leave the management of the affairs of the world ... to their betters; and now most of them were absolutely incapable of thinking of any abstract subject whatever. ... Therefore Crass and his mates, although they knew nothing whatever about it themselves, accepted it as an established, incontrovertible fact that the existing state of things is immutable. They believed it because someone else told them so. They would have believed anything: on one condition – namely, that they were told to believe it by their betters. They said it was surely not for the Likes of Them to think that they knew better than those who were more educated and had plenty of time to study. [**p 219**, p 203]

Perhaps it's becoming clearer why working-class students of my generation, who had been given time to study, could feel so suspicious of one of the most familiar and deeply effective modes in which we are indeed told what to believe by our betters.

The second danger is more subtle, even more implicit. It's not normally very effective at all simply to be told what to believe or what we should do. Tressell recognises this within his own fiction. At one point, for example, Owen runs up the stairs and since he has tuberculosis he's badly out of breath. His small son says, "How many times will Mother have to tell you about it before you take any notice?" [**p 88**, p 84] But though being told to do something or not to do something tend to be pretty ineffective as ways of actually changing behaviour, being told *not* to do anything at all or, even worse, being told that whatever you do will make no difference, can be decidedly effective. Arguably, the deepest convention of the novel is indeed that we as readers *can* do nothing, that the novel will take its course whatever we think or do, that its working through of its development and denouement is fundamentally 'inevitable' – is, indeed, beyond the control even of its author. The obverse of inevitability is, of course, passivity, acquiescence, a kind of surrender. A culture which so highly validates the process of merely 'following' a story tends, one might think, to produce mere followers. Again, much television can be seen as reinforcing older patterns here. But then simply telling people not to be passive or acquiescent, particularly in a mode which itself endorses passivity at another level, would surely be wholly ineffective. And that problem is endemic to any attempt to write a political novel which activates its readers towards a genuinely democratic mode of socialist politics.

How does Tressell negotiate these problems? Throughout the novel he poses precisely the difficulty, which Owen constantly faces, that no matter how many times you *tell* people about socialism, or that socialism is a good thing, or that they ought to become socialists, it has very little effect. But Tressell himself, though he uses – as I've tried to show – the normal devices of the traditional novelist, doesn't simply tell his own readers about socialism; nor does he manipulate the plot to 'demonstrate' the truth of socialism. Instead, he basically offers what I'll call exercises in understanding, which his readers can try out for themselves, within and beyond the text itself.

One obvious such exercise, which is almost an open invitation, is the passage where Hunter, as a fundamentalist preacher, is challenged on his claim that he believes every word of the bible. [**p 249**, p 231] Faced with Mark XVI – 'if they drink any deadly thing it shall not hurt them' – and a proffered bottle of strychnine, the blustering preacher rapidly backs off. Clearly, the reader is being invited to try the exercise on the next reactionary fundamentalist they come across.

Another obvious exercise is the Great Money Trick (ch. 21), when Owen demonstrates, by using three knives, three halfpennies and some bread, how the working class is exploited by the capitalist class. The reader is clearly being invited to try out the trick on his or her own mates: a trick to be taken out of the pages of the book and performed, rather than simply an argument to be analysed and repeated.

A third exercise is the chapter on the Oblong, where you are in fact given two exercises. The population of the country is divided into loafers, who simply exploit others, those who work but don't produce anything useful, and those who work and do produce useful things. It's an inevitable question, as you read, where you are to classify yourself. (I'm not sure about literary critics.) But that exercise is interrupted by another: we are given what we take to be Owen's hesitation and doubt:

> He knew they would refuse to try to see the meaning of what he wished to say if it were at all difficult or obscure. How was he to put it to them so that they would *have* to understand it whether they wished to or not. It was almost impossible.

> It would be easy enough to convince them if they would only take a *little* trouble and try to understand... [**p287**, p 266]

As a reader, I now have to classify myself as someone who is or isn't prepared to take a little trouble to understand.

The importance of these various exercises is that we are indeed being 'told' things, but in such a way that we have to think for ourselves about them. We are taken into the beginnings at least of a process of thought and inquiry, and not just given the result of that process – which is exactly how the Owens teach their own child within the novel. But isn't this just a palliative: aren't these moments just fragments of essay or treatise inserted into the novel? Isn't Tressell at these points trying to do what Perry Anderson claimed couldn't be done: to give us adequate concepts in ordinary language? And isn't he trying to do what Jack Mitchell implied shouldn't be done: to use a fictional form merely to get across a message?

At this point, let me backtrack to another aspect of both Anderson's argument and the great nineteenth-century novels: the ambition of 'totalisation'. Insofar as the nineteenth-century novels set out to totalise, to give a picture of the entire society, the essential formal problem was to find a focus for that total picture, some central point of intersection which was specific and plausible, which would act as a believable sampling or representative of the whole, where all the pressures and forces of the society might be seen as converging or revealed. There were various devices for this. One was to centre the novel on a particular character, and favourite candidates for this role in the nineteenth century were, for example, governesses, since they straddled several conflicting positions in the society, as both employee and intimate, as educated yet servant, and as female. The clergyman was another figure in whom several social pressures and determinants could be seen as intersecting. In the early twentieth century the favoured character upon whom to focus the entire novel and the entire society was often the artist figure himself. (To some extent, of course, Tressell's novel is a *Portrait of the Artist as an Artisan*)

Another kind of central focus would be an event: the novel would be structured round some crucial moment, an important historical event like 1848, or something as apparently minimal as a circus coming to town. Another organising focus might be a place, a courtroom, a boardroom, a country house. It's interesting to notice, as Jack Mitchell once pointed out, how often a house has acted as a focus for a novel. I started to pursue this, but realised that my talk at this point might turn into a whole WEA course! Think of *Wuthering Heights*, *Howards End*, *The Big House of Inver*, Shaw's *Heartbreak House*, *Bleak House*, Lettice Cooper's *The New House*, *Brideshead Revisited*, *A Doll's House*, *A House for Mr Biswas*, and more recently in America Gaddis's *Carpenter's Gothic* or Tracy Kidder's reportage *House*. The house has been offered as an embodiment of a whole mood and atmosphere, from Gothic mansions to Peake's *Gormenghast*; as a place where people meet to talk, as in W.H. Mallock's *The New Republic*; as a retreat outside social pressures or as the seething location of them. Think of the ideological role of Lutyens' revival of 'traditional' houses, or of Stately Homes and the Heritage industry today. One can think fairly easily of various familiar ways in which houses have been taken, within novels and in reality, as carriers or foci of meanings and values.

Arguably, Tressell's way of giving his novel its focus was deeply original. The houses in his novel, initially the Cave but then also others, are not just places where the action happens to occur, or where he brings together a variety of characters to have arguments. Nor does he merely use the house as a picaresque device, allowing his characters to move from house to house and thereby through a range of the society, though he does indeed do that. He also uses some of the houses emblematically, so that we see how Sweater's Cave contrasts so markedly in its wealth with the poverty-stricken houses of the men who worked to make the Cave so opulent. We're also brought to see, quite plainly, how the houses themselves are part of the system of exploitation: we're told very explicitly how much old Linden has paid out in rent to Sweater over the years, and how Rushton cheats those who commission the painting and decorating of the houses, by stealing from empty houses, by skimping and over-charging. All this is very plain and emphatic.

But Tressell goes further in two important ways. Since we are also given a direct account of the wage exchange which controls the work done by the men on these houses, and since the injustice of that wage exchange is clearly demonstrated by the Great Money Trick, we are led to see very precisely how it is the work done on the houses which generates the surplus for the bosses and the exploitation of the workers: the houses, as *work-places*, are clearly seen as a site of the fundamental exploitation which is at the centre of the whole social process – and to make the work-process as basic to a novel as it is to society was already to be deeply original.

But we are not only told this, or given a demonstration of how the analysis applies to the houses in the fiction. The choice of houses, of their building and repairing and decorating, as the focus of the novel, ensures that the whole novel acts as a kind of *reflexive exercise* upon the reader – since any reader almost certainly lives in some kind of a house. You cannot read this novel in a house without recognising that its analysis turns upon your own house, upon the very building in which you are reading it. Reading the novel, it's possible to pause and look, literally, at one's own walls for confirmation of its case. The novel makes you very conscious indeed that a house, any house, is the point where land, land-ownership, land values, finance, investment, interest, inflation, production, employment, labour, law, local government, national policy, individual need, hopes and possibilities, all converge in our daily experience. And that's true whether we rent, own or squat. It's true, also, though in a different way, of the building we're in at the moment. This Queens Hotel, like any building, is not only an emblem of the society we live in; it's also, in itself, a concretisation, an embodiment, of a process of exploitation, of a certain relation between capital and labour. One of the effects of this novel is that once you realise how houses are being used within the novel, you can't go down any street – because any street has some kind of houses in it – without having it brought literally *home* to you what the nature of capitalism is. I got off the train here an hour or so ago, and in the two minutes it took to walk down Havelock Street I passed seven estate agents, eight solicitors and the offices of several building societies.

It's now abundantly clear that housing has become, in the 1980s as in the 1880s, one of the crucial intersection points of the politics of our society, whether we think of home-ownership or the sale of council houses, the replacement of rates by a poll tax or the effect of mortgage interests (in both senses) on economic policies. Two fragments: one a report from the *Guardian*, 22 April 1988:

> Mrs Thatcher yesterday told a 73-year old widow who had lost all entitlement to housing benefit because of this month's Social Security changes that she should raise a loan against the security of her unsaleable terraced house in South Wales to help make ends meet.
>
> Deprived of housing benefits she is now left with £4 a week to live on. She has been unsuccessfully trying to sell her £15,000 house for 20 months.

Put this alongside a report a few days later (*Guardian*, 25 April 1988):

> The Government has discovered a source of income greater than privatisation, which has always been there, but which no one previously had dared to mine. It is called the poor.
>
> A recent paper written for stockbrokers Greenwell Montague states that if the earnings link had been retained married pensioners would now be getting £79.90 instead of £65.90. Greenwell estimates that the saving on State pensions this year will be a startling £4 billion.
>
> That £4 billion alone almost matches the income from privatisation proceeds and more than accounts for the £3.6 billion surplus in the Public Sector Borrowing Requirement.

Ragged Trousered Philanthropists indeed! It's one of the extraordinary achievements of Tressell's novel that it should speak so directly to our present political condition – and perhaps an indication of the inadequacy of the political perspectives into which it has been so often assimilated that it should still do so.

In focusing upon the house-building and decorating trade, Tressell resolved some of the major problems of the nineteenth-century novel: he found a focus which was not merely 'representative' of the whole society but genuinely had some immediate application to everyone within the society, and he constructed an organising centre for his novel which derived its persuasive power not from some manipulated plausibility of plot but from its fusion of emblematic suggestiveness and real referentiality. (Both solutions suggest a need for their political counterparts!) At one point within the novel he can both say:

> "Suppose some people were living in a house ------ " [**p 157**, p 145]

and go to elaborate an analogy between a badly built house and the present Money System, and then turn to the actuality of real, not emblematic, houses and argue:

> "In order that these people may live ... it is first of all necessary that they shall have a place to live in ... and that's the beginning of the trouble ... " [**p 160**, pp 148-9]

But of course that's only the beginning of the analysis you have to undertake as reader, to think through for yourself.

It's characteristic of that process, that exercise of thinking for yourself that, in the end, no one can think it for you. When I'd arrived at this point in my own argument, I happened to re-read Raymond Williams's foreword to Jack Mitchell's book, written in 1969. There, I found this typically compressed and laconic comment, which I had read long before but failed fully to grasp:

> Tressell draws much of his strength from the fact that his workers are a small and therefore immediately visible community and that their relationships to their employers and also to the general social system can be immediately dramatised in the house which they are decorating for somebody else – an unusually visible system of interlocking exploitation and social display. (p. xii)

That 'unusually visible system' is not, in practice, usually quite so visible to us. It's an important literary as well as political achievement of Tressell to make us see the houses all around us as, quite literally, visible evidence for the truth that is brought home to us by his wholly exceptional novel.

Notes on the Contributors

David Alfred was born in 1942 and brought up in west London. He graduated from Exeter University in 1963. He has taught in further education, and for the Oxford University Delegacy for Extra-mural Studies and the Open University. In 1979 he became Tutor-Organiser for the WEA South Eastern District. He convened the Robert Tressell Workshop which wrote and produced *The Robert Tressell Papers* (1982). He has written on *Political Education in the British Army, 1941-45* (dissertation, Surrey University, 1985) and on Albert Mansbridge (founder of the WEA) in *Twentieth Century Thinkers in Adult Education (ed. P. Jarvis,* 1987).

Tony Benn is the Labour Member of Parliament for Chesterfield. He has been an MP since 1950 and a member of the Labour Party's National Executive Committee since 1959. He was a Cabinet Minister in the four Labour Governments, 1964-70 and 1974-79. He has been chairman of the Fabian Society and prominent in the Peace movement and in campaigns for civil liberties, industrial democracy and the reunification of Ireland. He has written several books, including *Arguments for Socialism* (1979) and *Arguments for Democracy* (1981), and many pamphlets on various aspects of socialism.

Jack Jones was born in Liverpool in 1913. After leaving school at 14, he became an engineering apprentice, then a dock-worker. He served with the International Brigade in the Spanish Civil War. Later, he became a full-time official for the Transport and General Workers' Union. While he was General Secretary of the TGWU from his election in 1968 to 1977, he was prominent in the TUC, the architect of the conciliation service, ACAS, and joint chairman of the special Committee on the Ports (1972). In 1977 he gave the BBC Dimbleby Lecture on 'The Human Face of Labour'. He is co-author of *The A-Z of Trade Unionism and Industrial Relations.* Since his official retirement he has worked actively on behalf of pensioners' rights.

John Nettleton was born in Liverpool in 1940. He was active in the National Union of Seamen, becoming field organiser for the Seamen's Reform Movement and coordinator of ports. He worked for Courtaulds, becoming secretary of the Liverpool branch of the TGWU. During a spell of unemployment, he was chairman of the Merseyside Unemployed and a WEA/TUC tutor for unemployed activists. He is now a seaman on the Mersey ferries. He helped to found the Robert Tressell Museum in Walton, and co-authored the introduction to Jack Coward's pamphlet, *Back from the Dead.*

Raphael Samuel was born in 1934 and brought up in a Communist family. He has been Tutor in History at Ruskin College, Oxford since 1964. He was a founder of the 'New Left' in the late 1950s and of *History Workshop Journal* for which he is a co-editor . Author of many books and articles on social and labour history, he is now working on *Theatres of Memory*, a collection of historical and political writings, to be published by Verso in spring, 1989.

Bernard Sharratt was born in Liverpool in 1944. He graduated from Cambridge University in 1968. He is currently Reader in English and Cultural Studies at the University of Kent, where he has helped to set up new degree programmes in Film Studies, in Drama and in Psychoanalytic Studies. He is now organising a degree in Communication and Image Studies and writing a book on Yeats and Joyce. He has written *Reading Relations* (1982) and *The Literary Labyrinth* (1984) and co-edited *Performance and Politics in Popular Drama* (1980).

Raymond Williams was born in 1921 at the Welsh border village of Pandy. After graduating from Trinity College, Cambridge, he served in the Second World War as an anti-tank captain. After the war, he was Resident Tutor in Sussex for the Oxford University Delegacy for Extra-mural Studies. In 1961 he was elected fellow of Jesus College, Cambridge and in 1974 was appointed Professor of Drama. His many books include *Culture and Society* (1956), *The Long Revolution* (1961), *The Country and the City* (1973), *Keywords* (1976), *Politics and Letters* (1979), and four novels including *Border Country* (1960) and *The Volunteers* (1978). He died on 26 January 1988.

Norman Willis was born in 1933 and educated at Ashford County Grammar School and at Ruskin and Oriel Colleges, Oxford. He worked for the TGWU from 1949 to 1974, when he became Assistant General Secretary at the Trades Union Congress. He has been the TUC General Secretary since 1984 and has held a number of public and charitable posts, including membership of the NEDC, chairman of the National Pensioners Convention Steering Committee and an honorary vice-president of the WEA.

Eileen Yeo was born in New York City and came to England to research on her PhD at the University of Sussex where she now teaches history. She has written extensively on working-class and radical culture, particularly in the Chartist period. Over the years, she has been active in the Labour Party and in the QueenSpark community and publishing group in Brighton.